COVERING
the environment

A HANDBOOK ON
ENVIRONMENTAL JOURNALISM

By

MICHAEL KEATING

aussi disponible en français

National Round Table on the Environment and the Economy
Table ronde nationale sur l'environnement et l'économie

Canadian Catalogue Information in Publication Data
Covering the Environment - A Handbook on Environmental Journalism
(National Round Table Series on Sustainable Development)
ISBN 1-895643-20-1

Cover Design
Colton - Temple Design (613) 235-1044

This book is printed on Environmental Choice paper containing over 50% recycled content including 5% post consumer fibre using vegetable inks.The cover board also has recycled content and is finished with a water based, wax free varnish.
Printed and bound in Canada by Love Printing Service Ltd.

National Round Table on the Environment and the Economy
Table ronde nationale sur l'environnement et l'économie
1 Nicholas Street, Suite 1500, Ottawa, Ontario K1N 7B7

NATIONAL ROUND TABLE SERIES ON SUSTAINABLE DEVELOPMENT
1. Sustainable Development: A Manager's Handbook
2. The National Waste Reduction Handbook
3. Decision Making Practices for Sustainable Development
4. Preserving Our World
5. On the Road to Brazil: The Earth Summit
6. Toward Sustainable Communities
7. Trade, Environment and Competitiveness
8. The Green Guide - *A User's Guide to Sustainable Development for Canadian Colleges*
9. Sustainable Development - Getting There From Here
10. Covering the Environment - A Handbook on Environmental Journalism

Toutes publications de la Table ronde nationale sur l'environnement et l'économie sont disponible en français.

Series General Editor: Kelly Hawke Baxter
Tel:(613) 992-7189 Fax:(613) 992-7385

NATIONAL ROUND TABLE SERIES
ON SUSTAINABLE DEVELOPMENT

Canada

ABOUT THE AUTHOR

Michael Keating is an environment writer and consultant who was a newspaper reporter from 1965 to 1988, and environment reporter for The Globe and Mail from 1979 to 1988.

Mr. Keating wrote *Toward A Common Future*, the Canadian government's public discussion paper on sustainable development, which was released in 1989. He also wrote *The Report of the Task Force on the Environment* for The Canadian Chamber of Commerce, in 1989, and the report of Great Lakes Water Quality Board of the International Joint Commission, in 1991.

As a consultant, Mr. Keating has advised a number of government, business, environmental and other organizations at the national and international level. He founded and co-directs the Environmental Issues for Journalists short course at the University of Western Ontario. He is a director of the Canadian Global Change Program of the Royal Society of Canada, a member of the editorial board of the international journal, *ECODECISION*, and a member of the Commission on Environmental Strategy and Planning of The World Conservation Union. Mr. Keating is associated with the environmental studies programs at the University of Toronto and York University. He is a member of the Institute for Risk Research, and is an advisor for the Sustainable Society Project, both at the University of Waterloo.

Mr. Keating is the author of four other books: *To The Last Drop: Canada and the World's Water Crisis*, *Cross-Country Canada*, *Cross-Country Ontario* and *The Earth Summit's Agenda for Change*.

ACKNOWLEDGMENTS

This book owes its existence to the ideas and support of many people.

First, I want to offer special thanks for the work the late Thomas J. Royal, a communicator who first raised the idea of a course on environmental journalism, in 1989. This led to the creation of the Environmental Issues for Journalists course at the University of Western Ontario, and the writing of this book. Mr. Royal was a member of the Board of Advisors for that course.

The book has been produced, thanks to generous funding from the National Round Table on the Environment and the Economy, Ontario's Ministry of the Environment and the Laidlaw Foundation.

I want to offer special thanks for the initiative of Leone Pippard, a member of the National Round Table. Ms. Pippard is also a member of the Board of Advisors of the Environmental Issues for Journalists course.

I also want to thank Peter Desbarats, Dean of the Graduate School of Journalism, for inviting me to launch the Environmental Issues for Journalists course, and for his support for the handbook, which has been developed as a result of that course. Thanks also to Professor Colin Baird, codirector of the course, and without whom the project would never have succeeded. Professor Baird also provided valuable advice on chemistry for this book. I also want to thank the staff of The Centre for Mass Media Studies and Professional Development, Graduate School of Journalism, University of Western Ontario for their assistance in the course and production of the handbook. My thanks also goes to members of the Board of Advisors of the Environmental Issues for Journalists program for their advice on the course and handbook.

Iwould also like to give special thanks to staff members of the National Round Table and the Graduate School of Journalism for their assistance. In particular I want to thank Kelly Hawke Baxter of the National Round Table for her careful editing and her diligent work in getting the manuscript into print.

The writing of this book is the responsibility of the author, but it was only possible thanks to the help of many dozens of people who have provided their advice and insights over many years.

Finally, I offer many thanks to my wife, Nicole, for her great help and endless patience during the long writing process.

MICHAEL KEATING
Toronto, Ontario

FOREWORD

Journalism about the environment was a growth industry in the 1980s, and shows no signs of diminishing in the 1990s. In a world of multiplying populations and finite resources, our concern about environmental issues is bound to remain significant.

How we respond to environmental challenges will depend to a large extent on the information that we receive. News media play a major part in shaping our personal and political reactions to environmental problems.

This handbook recognizes the critical role of journalists in providing environmental information and the need to support them in the difficult task of interpreting complex environmental issues. A majority of journalists do not have scientific training. They are more at home with language than mathematics and chemical symbols; their networks of contacts rarely extend into the world of science.

This is particularly true of the political and business journalists, whose beats now bring them into regular encounters with environmental issues. Particularly in smaller news organizations, general assignment reporters and editors now find it a challenge to cover and handle environmental stories that require expert knowledge.

This handbook doesn't provide all the answers, of course, but it includes a compact encyclopedia or glossary of the most common environmental topics and terminology, guides to effective coverage of environmental issues, and a directory of useful contacts.

It is written for journalists by a journalist. The author, Michael Keating, was the environmental specialist for The Globe and Mail, Canada's national newspaper, before becoming an independent writer and consultant on environmental communications in Toronto.

Several years ago, Mr. Keating collaborated with Prof. Colin Baird, a member of the chemistry department of The University of Western Ontario, in launching a short course on environmental issues for professional journalists. With support from industry, government and environmental organizations, a prototype course was given to invited editors and news directors in 1991 under the auspices of the Graduate School of Journalism at The University of Western Ontario. A week-long course for reporters and editors is held each summer at Spencer Hall, Western's modern conference centre. Information about the course will be found elsewhere in the handbook.

The Environmental Issues for Journalists course is part of the Graduate School of Journalism's special commitment to professional development for Canadian journalists. Short courses are now offered annually at Western in law, economics and environmental issues, with new courses in medical and health journalism planned for the future.

Material for *Covering the Environment* was evaluated by journalists attending the 1992 course, and was prepared for publication in collaboration with the National Round Table on the Environment and the Economy. Additional funding for the handbook was provided by the Laidlaw Foundation and the Ontario Ministry of the Environment. Copies of the handbook in English and French are being provided to journalists, journalism schools and other interested groups across Canada.

PETER DESBARATS
Dean
Graduate School of Journalism
The University of Western Ontario
London, Ontario

PREFACE

The National Round Table on the Environment and the Economy (NRTEE) exists to advance environmentally sustainable development. (This is development that meets the needs of the present generation without compromising the ability of future generations to meet their own needs.) Given that in recent years our human activities have reached the same scale as natural processes, with devastating consequences on nature's ability to function, the achievement of sustainable development is becoming a paramount human challenge. There are many paths however to its realization. One very important one lies before the media.

In theory, the media mirror the world. But, by what the media choose to write about most, and comment on, the media also influence the public agenda. For example, in increasing its coverage on the environment in recent years, the media has played its own role in shaping public opinion about the state of our planet's health. In so doing it has influenced millions of citizens to be more concerned about the environment, plus to demand more action to restore and sustain it. It is this recognized power to influence the masses that confers on the media a special responsibility towards society. As such, if Canada and the world are to achieve environmentally sustainable development, what does this imply for the media?

The National Round Table asked journalists just that. They told us that in order to report on progress towards sustainable development they felt environment reporting would need to change. It would need to convey not only the outcomes flowing from human-induced environmental crises, but additionally it would need to analyse and explain the underlying development causes of those outcomes. That is, what unsustainable development policies, regulations, decisions, contributed to the problem's appearance and what would be different if more sustainable practises had been used.

They also felt business reporting would need to change to keep sustainable development in mind. It would require more of a focus on reporting whether or not the principles of sustainable development were being followed — in the formation of products and services, trade policies, etc. And where these principles are being followed, more good news reporting would serve to spread the knowledge of innovation to others.

As part of its efforts to explore with various sectors of Canadian society what moving to sustainable development means, the National Round Table on the Environment and the Economy was pleased to be involved in the development and publication of this handbook. *Covering the Environment* is Canada's first guidebook on environment and sustainable development issues written for journalists. It contains analyses of key issues, useful facts, figures and phone numbers, tips on coverage and lists of contacts who are helpful to working journalists. We hope that journalists will find this book a useful resource as they deal with the new challenges posed by the linkages between environment and economy issues in their reporting.

LEONE PIPPARD
Chair
Task Force on Education
National Round Table on the Environment and the Economy

TABLE OF CONTENTS

INTRODUCTION

Understanding the environment is not easy. Journalists are struggling with stories that involve a mix of atmospheric physics, organic chemistry, risk assessment, the use of natural resources, economics and politics. The journalist is bombarded with claims and counter-claims about the risk of a chemical, or the relative benefits of a major development such as a dam, forestry or energy project. A growing number of people claim that they, their political parties or their businesses are "environmentally friendly," and are practising sustainable development, but few journalists are equipped to weigh those claims.

Scientists can identify potential environmental problems long before anyone can tell the real effects. The journalist must try to understand the issues, and find a balance between overplaying or underplaying the potential risks. The media have a heavy responsibility, because they are the primary source of environmental information for most people. Environment stories influence government policies, corporate investments, educational programs and the shopping choices of millions of individuals.

Few journalists have any formal environmental or scientific education, and are forced to absorb complex ideas in the field and on the run. Most environment stories are not even covered by the environment beat reporter. They are handled by general assignment reporters and those who find them on their beats — City Hall, the Legislature, Parliament, business, science, mining, forestry and fisheries, for example.

This book is aimed not only at environment reporters, but it is also written so that other reporters and editors can find key facts, figures and references in a hurry. The material is a condensation of a great number of scientific reports from Canada and international agencies, along with useful facts, figures and phone numbers of contacts who are helpful to working journalists.

The first section outlines most of the major environmental issues, from acid rain to zebra mussels. The second gives a short outline of environmental journalism. The third is a reference section with a guide to scientific terms, a contact list for the media and suggestions about other sources. For in-depth coverage of issues, the journalist should refer to more specialized documents. One of the most useful reference books is *The State of Canada's Environment - 1991*, published by the Government of Canada, and sold in bookstores. Its 27 chapters contain the work of more than 100 experts from government, industry, universities and environment groups.

Although published in 1987, *Our Common Future*, the report of the United Nations sponsored World Commission on Environment and Development, stands as a major report on the environment and on the future of global development. It was the report that popularized the term "sustainable development," and launched a major advance in thinking about the root causes of and possible cures for environmental problems. It is often called the Brundtland Report after the commission chair, Dr. Gro Harlem Brundtland, prime minister of Norway. A shorter book that updates a number of the key ideas is *Beyond Interdependence,* co-authored by James MacNeill, who was secretary general to the Brundtland Commission. Both these books are published by Oxford, and are sold in bookstores.

Some other useful reference documents on environmental issues:

Health and Welfare Canada, *A Vital Link: Health and the Environment in Canada,* Ottawa, 1992. This book, sold in bookstores, deals with a broad range of health issues, including those linked to environmental problems.

Tolba, Mostafa K., *Saving Our Planet: Challenges and Hopes. The State of the Environment (1972-1992)*, Chapman and Hall, London, 1992. Sold in bookstores or through United Nations bookstore, New York, (212) 963-7680. This book is one of the best condensed reports on the state of the global environment.
Canada's Green Plan. This is a sort of master plan for dealing with major environmental problems in Canada. The Green Plan, released

in 1990, is to be implemented over five years. (See listings in Contacts section for Environment Canada communications officers.)

Toward A Common Future. This is the Canadian Government's public discussion paper on sustainable development, published in 1989. It is available free from Environment Canada communications offices.

Federal and provincial government departments, a large number of environmental, scientific and academic organizations, and a growing number of businesses and business groups provide excellent reports on a wide variety of issues. These can usually be obtained through communications offices of the organizations. There are also many excellent international reports, particularly those from the Worldwatch Institute and the World Resources Institute, both in Washington. A more detailed reading list is provided at the end of this book.

SECTION ONE
ENVIRONMENTAL ISSUES

THE NATURAL ENVIRONMENT

Our planet has always been in a state of change. The earth's crust cooled some 4.6 billion years ago, but for hundreds of millions of years the planet's environment remained hostile to life. The atmosphere was acidic, and it was bombarded by killing levels of ultraviolet radiation from the sun. The earth's surface was wracked by volcanic eruptions and was periodically pounded by meteors that have left great craters, visible even today. Then, water began to accumulate, forming the great oceans, and simple forms of life began to evolve in the sea between 3.5 and 4 billion years ago. Marine life produced oxygen as a waste by-product, and this gas began to form an atmosphere that could support air-breathing forms of life. As oxygen gathered in the atmosphere, some molecules were split apart by the sun's ultraviolet radiation, and they re-formed as ozone molecules. This created the stratospheric ozone layer high overhead that screens out most of the sun's harmful ultraviolet-B (UV-B) radiation before it reaches the earth's surface. This sunscreen allowed life to move out of the oceans and survive on land.

The development of life on earth has not followed a smooth pathway: 800 million years of fossil records found so far show 12 mass extinctions. During the last great extinction, about 66 million years ago, the dinosaurs vanished after ruling the earth for some 140 million years. With them went 60 to 80 per cent of species then on the planet. Mammals, which had been evolving in the shadow of the great reptiles for about 120 million years, began to flourish. Over the past 800,000 years, ice ages appear to have occurred roughly every 100,000 years, moving down from the north pole to cover large areas of North America, Europe and Asia.

There is evidence of smallish, human-like creatures, called hominoids, walking upright 3.7 million years ago. Modern humans (in the physical sense) existed in Africa about 100,000 years ago.

Societies that could produce magnificent wall paintings in the caves of what is now France and Spain, flourished at least 20,000 years ago. Permanent settlements with buildings and farms evolved in the last 10,000 years, since the end of the last ice age. The earliest known settlements are in what is now Iraq. Through most of human history, people lived with and adapted to a changing environment. With the first permanent settlements and farms, humans began to re-shape nature. By 3,500 BC, people were diverting rivers and irrigating crops in Mesopotamia, creating food surpluses and thus allowing the growth of cities. Ironically, cultivating the land, cutting large forests and herding too many animals on some pastures began what we now call environmental damage in the form of soil degradation. The fertile crescent between Tigris and Euphrates rivers in the Middle East was damaged by faulty irrigation practices which led to salinization of land thousands of years ago.

By now, human activity has begun to alter the environment on a global scale. Some chemicals are destroying the ozone layer, and a number of common pollutants are changing the natural layer of greenhouse of gases that keeps the planet at a stable temperature. Vast forests are levelled, and billions of tonnes a year of topsoil erode into the oceans. Thousands of species a year vanish from the face of the planet, never to return. Our impact on the planet is now visible from space. In the words of Canadian astronaut Marc Garneau: "The signs of life are subtle but unmistakable: sprawling urban concentrations, circular irrigation patterns, the wakes of ships, bright city lights at night and burning oil fields."

POPULATION AND CONSUMPTION — DRIVING FORCES OF CHANGE

There are two major forces driving environmental changes. The first is the sheer volume of human population growth. The second is the growing demand by people, especially in rich nations, for more of everything. At the dawn of agriculture, some 10,000 years ago, the world's population has been estimated at 4 to 5 million. By

2,000 years ago, it was possibly 200 million. The population explosion only began about three centuries ago. In 1650, there were about 500 million people on earth, by 1850 the world's population was 1 billion, by 1930 it was 2 billion, by 1960 it reached 3 billion, by 1975 it hit 4 billion and in 1987 it reached 5 billion. The world's population was 5.5 billion in 1992 and is growing rapidly. Every second, the net population increases by three people. That is 180 per minute, 10,000 per hour and about 95 million people a year, or nearly four Canadas. The United Nations forecasts that the world's population will reach 6 billion by 1998, 8 billion by 2020, and will climb toward 10 billion by the middle of the next century. Population experts say that given the large number of young people in the world now, there is little we can do to avoid the 8 billion level in less than 30 years. Only dramatic increases in family planning (or some disaster) will avoid the 10 billion level. Ninety per cent of the population growth is taking place in the poorer nations of the world.

Population and Energy

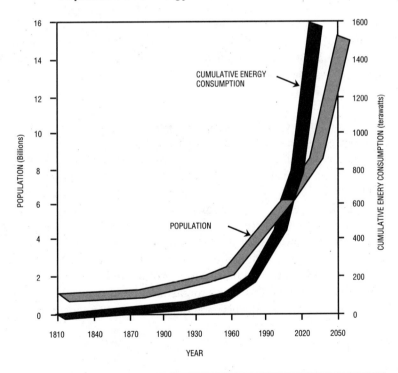

SOURCE: THE CANADIAN GLOBAL CHANGE PROGRAM

Simple population numbers do not tell the whole story about the scale of environmental change that lies ahead. Most economic activity and therefore most consumption and pollution has come from only one quarter of the world's population. The people who live in the world's 30 richest nations, generally in the northern hemisphere, consume 70 per cent of the world's energy, 75 per cent of its metals, 85 per cent of its wood and 60 per cent of its food. These nations also produce about 80 per cent of the world's pollution. It is estimated that the average Canadian consumes 50 times the resources of someone from a less industrialized nation. According to the United Nations Development Programme's 1992 report, the gap between the world's rich and poor doubled over the past three decades. The richest fifth of the world's population now receives 150 times the income of the poorest fifth. There are 1.3 billion people in the world without safe drinking water. Close to 1 billion people go to bed hungry every night, and hunger or infection kills 13 million children a year. The continent of Africa has not produced as much food as it has consumed since 1970. Poverty itself is an environmental threat. Not only do poor nations lack money to buy clean machines, but many people are so poor they must cut the remaining trees to cook and heat. They farm the soils and their animals graze the land too intensively because they are starving. At times, people even eat the seeds they will need to plant for next year's crop.

While many of today's poor will never consume a great deal, a number of the middle income nations are rapidly industrializing. The rate of economic growth in the world has been faster than the rate of population increase. Overall economic activity has grown 20-fold since 1900. In the same time period the use of fossil fuels grew by a factor of 30, and industrial production by a factor of 50. World population only grew about four times. In 1987, the Brundtland Commission forecast that if the global population doubles in the next half century, the world economy, now worth $13 trillion a year, will multiply 5 to 10 times. And it warned that if the new development was as environmentally blind as the old, it will create conditions "that the planet and its people cannot long bear."

State of the atmosphere

The atmosphere, the mix of clear gases that stretches for several hundred kilometres over our heads, is what we breathe and what creates the climate and weather patterns that govern our lives. This atmosphere is being changed by a mixture of industrial discharges, exhaust fumes, some agricultural practices and steady deforestation. This pollution is destroying the ozone layer, forming acid rain and adding more greenhouse gases to the air.

Climate change, global warming and the greenhouse effect

The atmosphere has long contained a natural level of such greenhouse gases as water vapour, carbon dioxide, methane and nitrous oxide. Short-wave radiation, including visible light from the sun, can pass through these greenhouse gases, warming the atmosphere, oceans, land and living creatures. Heat is radiated back into the sky in the form of long-wave infrared energy. Some of this infrared heat energy gets absorbed by greenhouse gases in the atmosphere and is re-radiated back to earth. Because of this natural greenhouse effect, we have a global annual average temperature of 15 degrees Celsius and what we consider a "normal" climate.

Human activities are injecting large amounts of such greenhouse gases as carbon dioxide, nitrous oxide, methane and chlorofluorocarbons into the air. According to a number of international scientific panels, the increased greenhouse effect will launch a planetary warming more rapid than anything in recorded history. This issue has been called global warming, climate change, climate warming, greenhouse effect and the enhanced greenhouse effect.

The greenhouse gases

• Carbon Dioxide (CO_2)
Since the industrial revolution began in the 1700s, the atmospheric level of carbon dioxide, the principal greenhouse gas emitted by humans, has risen from 280 parts per million to over 350 ppm, a

rise of 25 per cent. Human emissions of carbon dioxide account for about 55 per cent of the increased greenhouse potential in the atmosphere. CO_2 is a major by-product of the combustion of any fuel containing carbon. About 90 per cent of the commercially sold energy used in the world comes from carbon-based fuels: oil, coal, gas and wood. This releases about 6 billion tonnes of CO_2 per year. About 2 billion more tonnes of CO_2 are released by deforestation, including the burning of forests. *The State of Canada's Environment* report says that Canada releases 108 million tonnes of carbon per year. On a per person basis, each Canadian is responsible for four tonnes of carbon going into the atmosphere each year. According to *World Resources 1992-93*, a report of the World Resources Institute, this makes Canadians second only to Americans in per capita production of CO_2. About half the CO_2 released by humans is absorbed by plants on land and phytoplankton in the seas. The rest is added to the atmosphere.

Note: Figures for CO_2 emissions are given by weight, usually in tonnes. Sometimes the figure is only for the carbon component of CO_2, and sometimes it is for the total weight of carbon dioxide, including the carbon and oxygen. For example, 6 billion tonnes a year as carbon equals 22 billion tonnes as carbon dioxide. To convert from carbon to CO_2, multiply carbon by 3.66, and to convert from CO_2 to carbon, divide by 3.66.

The relative contribution of greenhouse gases to global warming during the past decade

The primary significance of carbon dioxide is apparent, but other gases, notably CFCs and methane, have grown in importance.

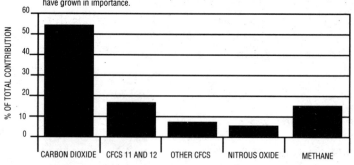

10

• Methane (CH_4)

Methane emissions contribute about 15 per cent of the increased greenhouse potential. Methane is the major component of the natural gas we burn in furnaces. This gas comes from decaying vegetation, such as that in water-logged rice paddies, bogs, swamps (swamp gas), the digestive tracts of a number of creatures, including cattle and termites, and the burning of vegetation where oxygen is limited. It also comes from leaks in gas mains, processing centres and appliances, coal mines, and decomposing organic material (such as food) in dumps. Researchers are concerned that some of the vast amounts of natural methane trapped under Arctic ice and in permafrost would be released by climate warming, creating what is called a feedback effect. This means that climate warming triggers effects which increase its rapidity.

• Nitrous Oxide (N_2O)

Nitrous oxide, one of the nitrogen oxides, comes from the burning of fossil fuels, the use of nitrogen fertilizers and the burning of trees and crop residues. It is responsible for about 6 per cent of the enhanced greenhouse effect. (Nitrous oxide is known as "laughing gas," and has been used as an anesthetic.)

• Ground level (tropospheric) Ozone (O^3)

In the stratosphere, high overhead, naturally created ozone acts as a screen against ultraviolet radiation. At ground level, ozone is a formed as by-product of the reaction of automobile and industrial air pollutants in the presence of sunlight. Ground-level ozone both attacks plants and animal tissue, and it acts as a greenhouse gas. It is estimated to be responsible for about 8 per cent of the enhanced greenhouse effect.

• Chlorofluorocarbons (CFCs)

Chlorofluorocarbons, chemicals that damage the ozone layer, are also potent greenhouse gases. Scientists are not certain of their actual effect on climate change, because their depletion of the ozone layer in the lower stratosphere may exercise a cooling effect on the planet. There is a possibility that reducing emissions of CFCs, which must be done to protect the ozone layer, may accelerate global warming. It is an example of how interconnected environmental issues are.

(In some documents you will run across comparisons of the greenhouse potential of various gases compared to CO_2. On a molecule for molecule basis, methane is 21 times more effective as a greenhouse gas, nitrous oxide is 206 times more potent and CFCs are up to 18,000 times more effective than CO_2.)

Predicted effects of climate warming

Scientists tend to refer to the impacts of global warming at a time when CO_2 levels in the atmosphere are "doubled." In fact, they are usually talking about a more than a simple doubling of CO_2 levels. They are referring to a time when the levels of all the greenhouse gases in the atmosphere are such that the net impact on the climate is the equivalent of a doubling of CO_2 from its pre-industrial level of about 280 parts per million. If the world continues to increase its emissions of greenhouse gases at the current rate, the "doubling" could take place between 2030 and 2050.

Environment Canada scientists predict that as this doubling occurs, the average global temperature will rise by 3.5 degrees, but there will be greater warming at the polar regions than near the equator. They estimate that for southern Canada, the warming would be about 4 to 5 degrees throughout the year, while in the north, the warming would be 8 to 12 degrees in the winter and 0 to 6 degrees in the summer. Southern Ontario will get a climate like Ohio and southern Alberta will be more like Nebraska. Even small changes in global average temperatures can have great effects. The world's average annual temperature 15,000 years ago, during the last ice age, was only 5 degrees cooler than now. Warmer temperatures would reduce heating costs, but would also increase the risk of droughts and the demand for energy to run air conditioners.

Global warming predictions:

- Scientists predict the seas will rise by about 6 centimetres per decade, mainly due to thermal expansion of the oceans and the melting of some glaciers. This would lead to a 20-centimetre rise by 2030, and 65 centimetres by the year 2100. Parts of Charlottetown would be awash, as would many heavily

12

populated deltas including those in Egypt and Bangladesh. A number of low-lying Pacific islands would be uninhabitable, and their leaders are pressing the world for controls on greenhouse gas emissions.

• Changes in rainfall and evaporation would result in less soil moisture in Southern Europe and central North America, two major food-producing areas. The Great Lakes could drop a metre or more. Tropical storms will likely become more powerful and destructive as ocean temperatures rise, and they may follow different paths.

• For each degree of global warming, forests will shift north about 100 kilometres. Scientists are worried that the warming will be so rapid that trees will have difficulty adapting. As habitats change, so will wildlife.

• More forest fires and insect infestations are expected in northern latitudes, such as in Canada, due to warmer temperatures and less summer moisture.

Variation of global mean surface air temperature since 1861

Values shown are departures of annual means from 1950-79 reference period mean

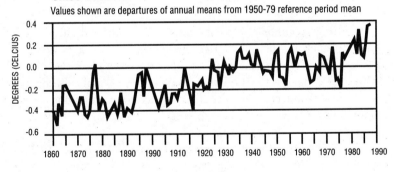

Reproduced with permission from:
Government of Canada, _The State of Canada's Environment — 1991_, Ottawa, 1991.

Is the earth getting warmer?

Over the centuries, the earth's average temperature has fluctuated by several degrees, possibly because of variations in heat given off by the sun. The average global temperature has increased about one-half degree Celsius since accurate measurements were started 1861. Canada's average annual temperature rose by 1.1 degrees between 1895 and 1991. According to Environment Canada scientists, this is within the limits of natural variability, but "consistent with predictions of global warming."

Controls on greenhouse gases

Experts meeting at the 1988 Toronto Atmosphere Conference said the world would have to cut CO_2 emissions by more than half just to stabilize the levels in the atmosphere. The meeting suggested that nations commit to a 20 per cent cut by the year 2005 as a starting point.

In 1990, the United Nations' Intergovernmental Panel on Climate Change said that in order to stabilize the levels of greenhouse gases in the atmosphere at 1990, levels the following emission reductions were needed:

Carbon dioxide	More than 60% cut
Methane	15-20% cut
Nitrous oxide	70-80% cut
CFC-11, CFC-12 and HCFC-22	40-85% cut

Cutting greenhouse gas emissions will be difficult, since most come from energy use and agriculture. Canada faces a particularly difficult task. We waste a lot of energy, but we are also a vast nation with long distances to travel and cold winters. We also produce a lot of raw resources, and this type of economy consumes large amounts of energy.

Virtually all nations have agreed to phase out the use of CFCs because they destroy the ozone layer, but only a few countries have made commitments to control CO_2 emissions. By 1992, a number of nations, including Australia, Austria, Belgium, Denmark, Germany, Netherlands, New Zealand had announced plans to slow or stop increases in CO_2 emissions. Canada is to stabilize emissions of CO_2 and other non-CFC greenhouse gases at 1990 levels by the year 2000. Several other nations, such as the United Kingdom, France and Finland, had a similar policy. Some large energy using countries, such as the United States and Russia, had not set specific control targets for CO2. The reality is that the world faces significant increases in greenhouse gas emissions, because it is impossible to make major cuts very quickly. Many experts are saying that we also need to develop adaptive strategies to deal with some of the impacts of a warmer world.

The ozone layer

The sun constantly bombards our planet with a wide spectrum of radiation, including the visible wavelength light we can see with the unaided eye, and invisible ultraviolet radiation: UV-A, UV-B and UV-C.

• UV-A, the weakest form of ultraviolet radiation, is still strong enough to cause sunburn, skin aging, and to damage plastics and paint. UV-A radiation is not stopped by the ozone layer, and most of it reaches the earth's surface.

• UV-B is stronger than UV-A. Some UV-B is healthy because it causes the body to form vitamin D. Too much UV-B causes sunburn, impairs the immune system, damages a number of crops and kills phytoplankton in the water. It also causes eye cataracts — a clouding of the eye which reduces vision. UV-B is partly blocked by the ozone layer, and by thick clouds. Less UV-B reaches the earth's surface when the sun is lower in the horizon, because some is stopped by water vapour and dust in the atmosphere.

• UV-C is stronger than UV-B, and potentially very destructive, but it virtually never reaches the earth's surface because it is filtered out by the atmosphere.

The ozone layer is 15 to 50 kilometres overhead, in the stratosphere. Ozone is continually being formed as UV-C radiation from the sun strikes oxygen (O_2) molecules — the kind of oxygen we breathe. Some O_2 molecules are broken apart and single O atoms combine with other O_2 molecules to form O^3, which is ozone. Some of those ozone molecules are destroyed by UV-B rays from the sun, or by other natural chemical reactions involving oxides of hydrogen and nitrogen. The amount of ozone that remains in the stratosphere acts as a filter which screens out most of the UV-B radiation before it can reach the earth's surface.

Over billions of years, the earth has evolved a natural thickness in the stratospheric ozone layer, and life on earth has adapted to a "normal" amount of UV-B radiation that reaches the surface. This amount is enough to cause sunburn and some skin cancer. Each year Canada has 3,200 new cases of the malignant skin cancer, known as melanoma, and 540 people die from it. There are also about 50,000 new cases of disfiguring by non-malignant skin cancers each year. Since cancer takes years to develop, medical experts say that most of the skin cancer we see today is probably the result of too much exposure to sunlight as a result of the tanning fad of the past few decades. Increased harm from a decline in the ozone layer will show up in the future.

One of the most dramatic aspects of the ozone story is the "hole" in the ozone layer that forms in Antarctica between September and November, then disappears. At times the area of reduced ozone is the size of the continental United States. A less dramatic ozone thinning has taken place periodically in the Arctic. In each case, the holes appear to be caused by high-altitude weather patterns that accelerate the degradation of the ozone layer for part of the year. Scientists have recorded a steady permanent decline in the ozone layer over most of the northern hemisphere. Above Environment Canada's major research station in Toronto, the ozone layer has declined by 6 to 8 per cent over the past 25 years, since significant destruction from CFCs likely began. Similar readings have been made in other parts of the northern hemisphere. Ozone depleting chemicals will remain in the atmosphere for decades to centuries, depending on the substance, so we can expect the ozone layer to keep thinning into the next century. In early 1992, a scientific advisor to the United Nations said there are about 20 million tonnes of CFCs in the atmosphere and another 3 million tonnes in use on the ground.

Chemicals that destroy the ozone layer

A number of industrial and household chemicals, particularly those containing chlorine and bromine, have the ability to float up into the stratosphere and cause ozone molecules to break apart. The damage begins when ultraviolet light splits apart the chemicals, releasing the chlorine or bromine molecules. A single chlorine molecule can destroy an estimated 100,000 ozone molecules before being washed out of the stratosphere. The major ozone destroying chemicals are: chlorofluorocarbons, halons, methyl chloroform, nitrous oxide, carbon tetrachloride and methyl bromide.

• Chlorofluorocarbons (CFCs)
This family of chemicals has hundreds of uses, including refrigeration, air conditioning blowing bubbles into various foam rubbers and plastics, sterilizing medical equipment and cleaning electronic equipment. In some nations, CFCs are still used as aerosol propellants. In Canada, the only aerosol use is for medical sprays such as asthma inhalers. CFC-11, CFC-12, CFC-113, CFC-114 and CFC-115 have been estimated to be responsible for about 70 per cent of stratospheric ozone depletion. The numbers following the letters CFC refer to the molecular structure of the chemicals and indicate the purpose they will be used for. CFCs 11 and 12 have been the most commonly used. Canada has an estimated $15 billion of equipment, mainly refrigerators and air conditioners, that run on CFCs, and the global figure is $200-$250 billion. A typical refrigerator uses 0.22 kilograms (one-half pound) of CFC-12 as coolant circulating in the tubing found behind most refrigerators, but at least 1 kilogram of CFC-11 is in the bubbles in the foam insulation. Various CFCs are also found in the flexible foam in furniture and some rigid foams in wall insulation.

There are so called "hard" and "soft" CFCs. The "hard" CFCs, such as CFC-11, CFC-12 and CFC-113, have a high potential to deplete the ozone layer because they resist natural breakdown in the lower atmosphere, and carry their chlorine molecules high into the stratosphere. Some of the replacement chemicals on the market are called "soft" CFCs, because they will break down more quickly in the lower atmosphere, and thus have less potential to carry chlorine into the stratosphere, where it can damage the ozone layer. The

17

major "soft" chemical replacements for CFCs are the hydrochlorofluorocarbons (HCFCs) in which a hydrogen atom is added to the CFC molecule to help the molecule break down in the lower atmosphere. The breakdown is not complete, and HCFCs are estimated to have between one and five per cent of the ozone depleting potential of CFCs. HCFCs are now being used in a number of air conditioners, heat pumps, refrigerators and foam-blowing applications. Environment Canada says that because they have some ozone-depleting chemical, HCFCs must be seen as temporary replacements for CFCs.

• Halons
Halon gas is chemically similar to CFCs, except halons contain bromine molecules, and this chemical is three to six times more effective at destroying ozone than chlorine. Halons are used in a number of fire extinguishers, especially in aircraft and computer rooms.

• Carbon tetrachloride
This industrial solvent is used to remove grease from metals and electronic equipment. It is also an agricultural insecticide, and a chemical used in a large number of industrial processes. Most carbon tetrachloride is used in the production of CFCs and similar chemicals. In some countries it is still used as a dry-cleaning fluid.

• Methyl chloroform
This is another industrial solvent used to remove grease from metals and electronic equipment. Methyl chloroform is also used in aerosols, coatings and adhesives.

• Nitrous oxide
This is one of the nitrogen oxides that are formed by high-temperature combustion, and the decay of agricultural fertilizers. There has been concern that nitrogen oxides from the engines of very high-flying aircraft could damage the ozone layer.

• Methyl bromide
This is a highly toxic pesticide used to fumigate soil and food storage areas. It releases bromine, which is more destructive to the stratospheric ozone layer than chlorine.

Effects of UV-B radiation

For every 1 per cent decrease in the ozone layer, there is about a 1.2 per cent increase in the amount of UV-B radiation reaching the ground. United Nations experts calculate that for every 1 per cent decrease in the ozone layer, there will be 100,000 more blind people in the world, because of eye cataracts. There will also be 50,000 more non-melanoma skin cancers. The head of the United Nations Environment Programme said in 1992 that a sustained 10 per cent decrease in the ozone layer could lead to a 26 per cent increase in non-melanoma skin cancers. UV-B radiation can also suppress the immune system, leading some experts to say we face the risk of more infectious diseases and a reduction in the effectiveness of vaccinations.

UV-B radiation harms such major food crops as cotton, rice, corn, beans, peas, soybeans, cabbages and lettuce. Experiments show a 1 per cent depletion of the ozone layer causes a 1 per cent reduction in the crop yield of soybeans. The rays can injure or kill phytoplankton, zooplankton, small crabs, shrimp and fish in the upper layers of the ocean — creatures at the base of the oceanic food chain. Scientists have reported reductions of phytoplankton in Antarctic waters. In Australia and New Zealand, children are frequently warned to stay out of direct sunlight during periods of increased UV-B radiation. The radiation will also magnify the effects of pollution from motor vehicles by speeding up the formation of smog.

Canada's UV index

Canada has an Ultraviolet Advisory Program to let people know how much UV radiation they face outdoors. The UV index predicts the intensity of the sun's ultraviolet rays on different parts of the country each day under clear sky conditions. The actual amount of radiation reaching the ground varies, depending on the season, latitude, time of day and such other variables as cloud cover and the state of the ozone layer. Readings are given on a scale of 0 to 10. The maximum reading of 10 represents the typical UV intensity on a clear, sunny day in the tropics with a normal ozone layer overhead.

The scale gives the predicted intensity of both UV-A and UV-B radiation. Health experts say that UV levels are greatest at midday in mid-summer, when the sun is most directly overhead in Canada. Haze and thin clouds do not screen out UV-B, but thick clouds do. Dermatologists recommend using a sunscreen with a Sun Protection Factor (SPF) of at least 15 on skin exposed to intense sunlight.

Typical mid-summer UV levels on a clear, sunny day at solar (not daylight saving time) noon at different latitudes are:

Region	UV index	Sunburn risk
Tropics	10	extreme
Washington D.C.	8.8	high
Toronto	8.0	high
Edmonton	7.0	high
Yellowknife	6.0	moderate
Iqualuit	4.8	moderate
North Pole	2.3	low

Approximate time for a fair-skinned, untanned person to get a sunburn:

UV index	Category	Sunburn time
9-10	extreme	less than 15 minutes
7-9	high	about 20 minutes
4-7	moderate	about 30 minutes
0-4	low	more than one hour

Controls on ozone-depleting chemicals

In the mid-1970s, after the first warnings that CFCs could attack the ozone layer, consumer boycotts in North America and parts of Europe, especially the Nordic nations, led to reductions in their use in aerosol sprays. The 1985 Vienna Convention for the Protection of the Ozone Layer led to the 1987 Montreal Protocol on Substances that Deplete the Ozone Layer. This protocol required signatory nations to achieve a 50 per cent cut in the use of CFCs 11, 12, 113, 114 and 115 by mid-1998. They were to freeze the use of halons

1301, 1211 and 2402 at 1986 levels by 1992. In November 1992, nations meeting in a follow-up to the Montreal Protocol agreed to eliminate new CFC uses by the end of 1995, and to discontinue the use of halons by the end of 1993. They said there should be a phased reduction of HCFCs from 2004 to 2030. By late 1992, world-wide consumption of CFCs had dropped to about 500,000 tonnes a year from the 1 million tonnes a year of the mid-1980s. The Canadian supply of all ozone-depleting chemicals, including CFCs, dropped by more than 50 per cent from 1987 to 1991 to reach a level of 13,000 tonnes.

Alternatives to CFCs and HCFCs

Some companies found alternatives to the use of CFCs by changing the way they produce goods. Hydrocarbons such as pentane (a refined form of butane) are replacing CFCs as aerosol propellants and foam-blowing gases. Some electronic companies that used CFCs as solvents to clean electronic parts, such as computer chips, are now washing parts with water or with substances such as lemon juice. Northern Telecom Ltd. of Mississauga, Ontario, pioneered ways of making electronic parts that do not need intensive cleaning. By early 1992, the new technology had cost Northern Telecom $1 million, but had saved it $4 million in chemical bills. It is sharing this technology with other companies, including those in developing countries.

Note: In scientific reports and satellite images of the ozone layer, the term Dobson Unit (DU) is used to indicate the thickness of the ozone layer. The normal thickness of the stratospheric ozone layer is 350 DU. Anything less represents a thinning of the layer.

Acid rain

Acid rain, more properly called acid precipitation, has been recognized as a serious threat to Canada's environment since the mid-1970s. The pollution begins as colourless gases that pour from millions of chimneys, smokestacks and exhaust pipes to travel tens, even hundreds of kilometres before falling to earth as dry particles, fog, snow and rain. The main acid gases are sulphur dioxide (SO_2) and nitrogen oxides (NO_X).

The most serious acid fallout damage in Canada is caused by sulphur dioxide. Most of it comes from burning sulphur-containing coal to generate electricity, and smelting (burning) sulphur-bearing ores to separate such valuable metals as nickel, copper and zinc. In the boilers and smelters, sulphur combines with oxygen from the air to form sulphur dioxide. In the atmosphere this is converted to sulphate (SO_4) and sulphuric acid. Nitrogen oxides are by-products of high temperature combustion, in which nitrogen from the air combines with oxygen from the fuel or air to form a chemical combination— usually nitric oxide. Once it gets into the air it is rapidly converted to nitrogen dioxide, then to other substances such as nitric acid, ammonium, ammonium nitrate and nitrate.

Acidity is measured on the pH scale that runs from 0 to 14, with 7 being neutral. Anything below 7 is acidic and anything above is alkaline. This is a logarithmic scale, which means that every unit of measurement is ten times greater than the next. Thus, pH 6 is 10 times more acid than pH 7. A reading of pH 5 is 100 times more acid than pH 7, and a reading of pH 4 is 1,000 times more acidic than neutral. When the pH of lakes and rivers falls below 6, such species as crayfish and mayflies begin to decline and may die out, and below pH 4.5, fish die out. The rain falling on southern Ontario and Quebec and into the Atlantic provinces is commonly in the pH range of 4.2 to 4.5. Over time, this constant acid fallout uses up the natural buffering capacity of soils, especially in areas such as the Precambrian Shield, which has little natural buffering capacity. Limestone and alkaline soils are a natural buffering agent. The corrosive fallout has already damaged an estimated 150,000 of 700,000 lakes in eastern Canada. About 14,000 lakes are believed by scientists to be acidified, which means they are losing normal aquatic life, including fish, ducks and amphibians, by interfering with reproduction or with food supplies. Acidic air pollution has been linked to the decline of some forests.

Tiny droplets of acid, known as aerosols, can attack the respiratory system. Acid rain also dissolves harmful metals from the rocks and plumbing, putting them into the food chain and some drinking water supplies. Acid rain is eating away at the monuments civilization. The Acropolis of Greece, statues in Rome, cathedrals of Europe, the Taj Mahal of India, Mayan temples in Mexico, the Statue of Liberty and the Parliament Buildings are all discolouring, peeling and eroding. Acidic damage to cars, buildings, bridges and monuments costs Canada about $1 billion a year.

Most of the sulphur dioxide emissions in eastern Canada come from smelters, particularly six big ones in Ontario, Quebec and Manitoba, and from about 20 coal and oil-burning power plants in Ontario and the Atlantic provinces. In western Canada, the acid gas sources are mostly oil and natural gas centres. In the Prairies, soils are more alkaline and better able to buffer the acids. In the United States, about half the sulphur comes from more than 400 coal-burning power plants and industrial boilers, especially in the industrialized midwestern states of the Ohio River valley. The main sources of nitrogen oxides in both nations are motor vehicles, furnaces and power plants. There are about 12 million motor vehicles in Canada and more than 140 million in the United States. Canadian government researchers say that about half the sulphuric acid rain falling on Canada has been blowing north from the United States.

After long and often heated public debates during the 1980s, Canada and the United States introduced major acid gas control programs, particularly for sulphur dioxide.

• In the acid-sensitive eastern part of the nation, Canada is cutting its allowable sulphur dioxide emissions from 4.5 million tonnes in 1980 to 2.3 million tonnes in 1994. The next stage is to establish a national cap on sulphur dioxide at 3.2 million tonnes a year.

• Canada is to reduce its nitrogen oxide emissions by 10 per cent from the 1.9 million tonnes of 1980.

• The revised U.S. Clean Air Act will reduce the emissions of sulphur dioxide in that country by about 10 million tonnes by the year 2000, a 40 percent reduction from 1980 levels.

23

• The U.S. program will cut about 2 million tonnes of nitrogen oxides from 1980 levels by the year 2000.

In order to meet the new pollution standards, electric utilities use air pollution control devices called scrubbers, burn low-sulphur coal and use new forms of combustion. Scrubbers spray fine limestone into waste gases to capture the sulphur before it goes up the smokestack. Power plants will also use low nitrogen burners. Metal smelters are being modernized with cleaner technologies, or are using equipment to remove sulphur from the ore or scrub it from the smokestacks. Cars will use better pollution control technologies to reduce nitrogen oxides, which form both acid rain and urban smog, and to control other air pollutants.

Allowable sulphur dioxide emissions (in million metric tonnes)			
	1980	1994-95	2000
Eastern Canada	4.5	2.3	2.3
United States	24.3	17.8	14.1

By August 1991, sulphur dioxide emissions in eastern Canada were down by about 40 per cent from 1980 levels. The federal government position is that a 50 per cent cut in sulphur gas emissions will reduce fallout on almost all of Canada to no more than 20 kilograms of wet sulphur per hectare per year (2 grams per square metre). They say this will prevent damage to moderately sensitive ecosystems. In late 1992, the Commons environment committee said that further reductions were needed. It said that some parts of Canada, such as New Brunswick, were getting almost four times more acid fallout than their aquatic ecosystems could absorb without harm.

Long-range toxic fallout

"After an orange cloud — formed as a result of a dust storm over the Sahara and caught up by air currents — reached the Philippines and settled there with rain, I understood that we are all sailing in the same boat." — Soviet Cosmonaut Vladimir Kovalyonok.

Acid rain is not the only form of long-range transport of air pollutants (LRTAP in scientific jargon). There are PCBs and pesticides in penguins, polar bears and every human tested in the world, due to the phenomenon of long-range transport. Great invisible rivers of air pollution carry heavy metals, industrial chemicals and pesticides across the sky to fall on urban and rural areas alike. Fallout from the 1986 explosion at the Chernobyl nuclear power plant in the former Soviet Union showed that pollution can circle the planet in 11 days.

Pollution from North America, Europe and the former Soviet Union forms a brownish-yellow Arctic haze. The Arctic snow pack contains agricultural and industrial chemicals including PAHs, Lindane, dieldrin, toxaphene, heptachlor epoxide, chlordane, DDE, PCBs, lead and Endosulfan. These are mainly pesticides that have been used thousands of kilometres to the south. Researchers have found elevated levels of PCBs and some other chemicals in the milk of nursing mothers in the Arctic. Some of the chemicals in the Arctic food chain are carried north from industrialized areas on ocean currents or in north-flowing rivers, but most of this long-range transport is likely through the atmosphere. Some chemicals and fine metal particles are injected into the sky by tall smokestacks or carried on fine dust particles blown off fields where farm chemicals have been sprayed. Other chemicals evaporate into the sky just as spilled gasoline dries on the hot metal of a car on a sunny day, almost faster than it can be wiped.

Smog

Smog is a combination of smoke and fog. It is also known as photochemical haze. Smog has a characteristic brownish colour that comes from nitrogen dioxide, a by-product of combustion at high temperatures, as in car engines and power plants. Smog also contains dozens of other chemicals created when nitrogen oxides react with volatile organic compounds (VOCs) in sunlight. VOCs include unburned hydrocarbons (gasoline) from motor vehicles as well as chemicals released by industries, dry cleaners and even backyard barbecues.

Ground-level ozone (or bad ozone as some scientists call it) makes up 90 per cent of photochemical smog. The ozone is created when UV-A rays from the sun strike nitrogen dioxide, splitting off one oxygen atom, which quickly combines with an oxygen molecule (O_2) to form ozone (O^3). Ozone is above acceptable levels in Windsor, Sarnia, Toronto and Montreal for an average of 16 days each summer. It is also a problem in Vancouver and the lower Fraser Valley, and in Saint John, N.B. The acceptable level is 82 parts per billion over one hour. Ground-level ozone attacks the respiratory system, can cause a decrease in the effectiveness of lungs, and can aggravate other lung ailments, such as asthma and pneumonia. Ozone also causes damage to a number of plants, and has reduced yields of some Southern Ontario crops by up to 12 per cent.

STATE OF THE LAND

Forests

Forests are a key part of the global air conditioning system, for without trees there can be no rain and without rain there can be no trees. Trees, like other green plants, suck carbon dioxide out of the sky, use the carbon to build themselves, and release oxygen. Thus they combat the increased greenhouse effect. Forests, especially those in the tropics, are home to many of the known species of life on earth, and deforestation is leading to the loss of many forms of life. In the past two centuries, the world has lost one fifth of its original forests. Tropical forests, which include moist tropical forests (rain forests), cloud forests (at higher altitudes) and dry tropical forests, are being cut or burned at the rate of about 170,000 square kilometres a year, an area more than three times the size of Nova Scotia. In 1987, the Brundtland Commission estimated that, at the then current rate of loss, only forests in parts of central Africa, South America and New Guinea would remain uncut by early in the next century. That commission said the world needed to plant trees on an area the size of Saskatchewan every year to counter forest losses.

Nearly half of Canada, more than 4.5 million square kilometres, is forested. The nation has about 10 per cent of the world's forests by area and about 7.5 per cent by volume, but only half our timber is close enough to roads and mills to be commercially usable, and that is the part that is being cut. Forest industries are a major part of the economy. In 1989, they employed about 293,000 Canadians and shipped goods worth $50 billion.

Canada is the world's:
- largest exporter of forest products
- largest producer of newsprint
- second-largest producer of wood pulp
- third-largest producer of softwood lumber

Forestry has become highly controversial in the past decade. Almost 90 per cent of logging in Canada is carried out by clear-cutting, which means felling virtually every tree in a given area, often called a cut block. Forest companies say this is economically efficient, and mimics natural destruction of large forest tracts by fire and insects. Many environmentalists say clear-cutting is too destructive of the environment, and it leads to the decline in species, soil erosion and the fouling of streams by silt and branches. There is also a heated debate about the preservation of old-growth forests, which are essential habitat for a number of species, including the spotted owl and marbled murrelet in the Pacific northwest.

Canadians plant about one billion tree seedlings a year, about twice the number of trees cut. Despite a great increase in replanting trees in recent years, many areas of Canada are facing wood shortages. Canada's most valuable trees, spruce and pine, take 50 to 75 years to grow to a commercial size in most of the country. Even when the planted trees are ready to harvest, many will lack the wood quality of trees that have grown over centuries. This decline in wood quality is called the falldown effect, particularly in British Columbia, home of very big and old trees.

Another problem for the forest industry is its discharge of chemical wastes from pulp and paper mills. There is pressure for mills to reduce or even stop using chlorine to bleach paper to a white color desired by many people. Chlorine reacts with other chemicals and components of wood to produce a host of chlorinated organic compounds, including dioxins and furans. The pulp and paper industry is facing increasingly tough regulation, and expects to invest around $4 billion during the 1990s to upgrade plants to meet new federal and provincial pollution standards. Canadian pulp and paper mills are also facing competition from recycled paper, for which there is a growing market. However, de-inking of old paper produces its own chemical wastes.

Degrading the land

"Land degradation, in the form of soil erosion, soil salinity and related problems, has faced humans ever since land was first settled and cultivated at least 7,000 years ago. It has caused or contributed to the decline of great civilizations in such places as China, Mesopotamia, Egypt, North Africa and Greece." — D.W. Sanders, in The Journal of Soil and Water Conservation, September-October 1990.

As forests are depleted and grasslands over-grazed or farmed too intensively, the land is degraded in a process often referred to as desertification. One third of the planet is already desert, of which 6 per cent is extremely dry and the rest is arid to semi-arid, with some plant cover. Deserts of various kinds are spreading at the rate of 60,000 square kilometres a year, an area larger than Nova Scotia and Prince Edward Island together. When one adds the effects of waterlogging, salinization, alkalization and soil compaction from bad farming practices, the amount of land damaged rises to about 80,000 square kilometres yearly.

About 20 per cent of Canada's farmland is deteriorating. The Prairies alone lose 300 million tonnes of soil a year to erosion, and they have lost half their organic matter and biomass since the land was first broken. Canada is also losing an estimated 100 square kilometres of its most productive farmland every year to urbanization. Most of it is in the best growing regions, such as southern Ontario, the St. Lawrence lowlands of Quebec and the fruit and vegetable growing regions of British Columbia.

Parks and wilderness

Canada has the image of a land of wilderness. In the north, there are still vast, wild areas, but in the heavily populated southern areas, wild lands are one of the fastest disappearing resources.

• Wilderness retreated 100 kilometres from Montreal and Toronto during the 1980s.

• Only scattered remnants of the Carolinian forest are left in southern Ontario.

• Only 2.6 per cent of the old-growth forest on the Pacific coast of British Columbia is protected. Most of the rest is slated for clear-cutting over the next 20 years.

• More than 99 per cent of the original tall-grass prairie has been plowed, and the largest remnant is 10 hectares in a park within the Winnipeg city limits. In addition, 82 per cent of short-grass prairie, 90 per cent of fescue grassland and 76 per cent of mixed-grass prairie and aspen parkland have been turned into farms, pastures or cities.

• The original Acadian forests of the Maritimes are almost gone.

• More than half the original wetlands of southern Canada are gone. This includes 65 per cent of the Atlantic coastal marshes, 70 per cent of wetlands in southern Ontario and Quebec, including 90 per cent of those in southwestern Ontario, and 80 per cent of the Fraser River Delta wetlands. Western wetlands, among the richest in the world, have shrunk by 27 to 61 per cent, depending on the area, and are being drained at the rate of 11 to 21 per cent a year.

Canada's first protected areas were municipal parks, such as Mount Royal in Montreal, and the first national park was Banff, created in 1885. According to *The State of Canada's Environment* report, between 65 and 72 per cent of Canada is still wild, but wilderness declined by 4 per cent, an area greater than all the country's national parks together over the last 15 years. Just over 7

29

Urban settlements in Canada

The population distribution in Canada by census division for 1986 is shown.
Each dot represents 1,000 persons.

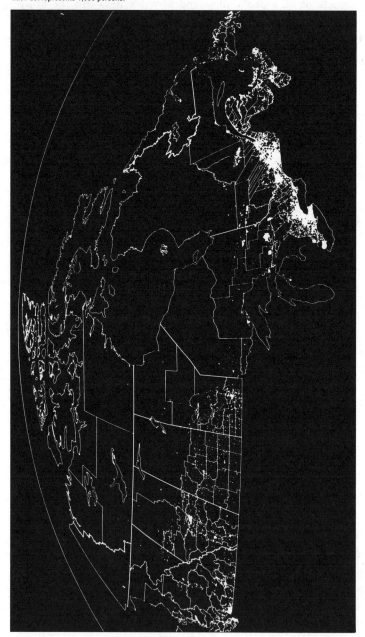

Reproduced with permission from: Government of Canada, *The State of Canada's Environment — 1991*, Ottawa, 1991.

per cent of Canada is set aside by all governments as parks, wildlife areas and ecological reserves. World Wildlife Fund Canada (WWF) has promoted the Brundtland Commission's recommendation of protecting 12 per cent of the world for conservation, and said it should be adopted as Canada's goal. In late 1992, Canada's environment and parks ministers agreed with the 12 per cent target. WWF Canada said that only 4.6 per cent of the country had been protected from extractive uses, such as logging, mining and hydro-electric development. Some of the "wild" parks and protected areas allow hunting, motorboats and fly-in camps.

STATE OF THE WATERS

Our world appears as a blue planet in photographs taken from space — 70 per cent of it is covered with water. When it comes to human needs, that image is deceptive. Less than one one-hundredth of one per cent of all water is fresh and readily available in lakes, rivers and shallow wells. Around the globe, there is a growing series of water crises as people over-use their local sources. This is particularly the case in developing countries, where 90 per cent of population growth will take place in coming decades. Under present trends, two thirds of Africa will be without adequate water supply by the year 2025. Politicians from both Israel and Egypt have warned that the next war in the region is likely to be over fresh water.

The popular image of water use is a flushing toilet or dripping tap. Over-use of water in towns and cities causes problems in some areas. About 70 per cent of the water consumed at a global level — taken from a lake, river or underground aquifer and not returned — is used for agricultural irrigation. On average, 60 per cent of the world's irrigation water is wasted. Inefficient techniques let it evaporate into the sky or run right by the plants, without reaching their roots. The water is consumed in that it evaporates and is blown away from the region, or it seeps into the ground and does not return to lakes and rivers, thus dropping their levels. One of the most dramatic cases of over-use, is in the south-west portion of the former Soviet Union. So much water has been taken from tributaries of the Aral Sea, mainly to irrigate crops like cotton, that the Aral's surface area has shrunk by 40 per cent and its volume by 60 per cent.

Around the world, water pollution is a growing problem. According to the United Nations Environment Programme, about 10 per cent of the world's rivers are heavily polluted, and a significant number are virtually dead or dying. More than one billion people lack access to safe drinking water, and water-borne diseases kill 25,000 people a day, mainly children in poor countries. More than half the world lacks proper sanitation for human wastes.

Canada, with about 14 per cent of the world's lake water, 9 per cent of river flow, and less than one-half of one per cent of the global population, is water rich. Canadians are the world's second-largest consumers of water per person, after the United States. Like the story of wilderness, the water story is deceptive. Most of Canada's rivers flow north, but the demand is in the south. Canada has a number of regional shortages, particularly in the Prairies and southern Ontario.

Pollution is a serious problem in a number of regions. Scientists have found 362 contaminants in the Great Lakes ecosystem, including the water, sediments, fish, animals, waterfowl and humans. The list includes 126 substances that cause illness to wildlife or humans. The Science Council of Canada reported in 1988 that as many as a million Canadians may already be risking their health by drinking well water that is contaminated by human or animal wastes, fertilizers or farm pesticides.

Although most municipal water meets all government guidelines (usually not enforceable laws), many people do not trust tap water. A 1990 survey showed 20 per cent of Toronto residents used bottled water regularly instead of tap water. "This reflects a growing perception among the public that drinking water is increasingly contaminated with pollutants and therefore unsafe," according to *The State of Canada's Environment*. Several studies have found that some bottled waters contain a number of contaminants. Home water filters need regular maintenance and replacement of parts, or they may become breeding grounds for bacteria, or may release the chemicals they have been collecting.

There is a hot debate over the preservation of wild rivers. More than half Canada's major rivers have been dammed, and many others are being considered for dams to generate hydro-electricity. Although hydro-electricity is described as "clean energy," the dams disrupt the environment in several ways. The water trapped behind giant hydro dams has caused increased levels of mercury in fish in parts of Manitoba and Quebec. Microbes that thrive in the presence of drowned organic matter can transform naturally occurring inorganic mercury into toxic methylmercury, which then gets into the food chain. This has led to restrictions on the amount of fish that people should eat, and has disrupted traditional lifestyles and diets. Big dams have also disrupted water levels, reducing wildlife habitat in a number of areas. One of the major examples is that of the Peace-Athabasca delta in the Northwest Territories, one of the world's largest freshwater deltas, and a major waterfowl breeding area. The W.A.C. Bennett dam in British Columbia has changed the normal flows of the Peace River so much that the delta is gradually drying up.

Since the 1960s, there have been proposals for massive water diversions from Canada to the United States and as far as Mexico. One plan would divert Alaskan rivers through the Rocky Mountains by flooding the Rocky Mountain Trench. Another would dyke James Bay, and pump water through the Great Lakes and then by canal to western Canada, the United States and Mexico. According to a number of water experts, diversions will not be necessary if people use serious water conservation techniques. These range from water-efficient shower heads and toilets in homes to highly efficient irrigation and industrial water-use systems.

STATE OF LIFE ON EARTH

As humans push back the forests and marshes of the world, the habitat disappears for other species, and they are disappearing faster than they can be counted. So far, biologists have catalogued 1.4 million species of life, including plants, insects, fish, reptiles, animals and birds. Scientists estimate that there are at least 5 million and possible 10-30 million more species on earth. Most are waiting to be discovered in the tropical and semi-tropical forests and swamps, or on tropical reefs. One 50 square kilometre site in Peru supports 500 bird species while Canada, with 10 million square kilometres, has only 426 known breeding birds. About 700 species of trees have been identified in a 15 hectare area of Borneo rain forest, more than all the tree species in North America.

According the Worldwatch Institute, the "normal" rate of extinction in the past was 1 to 10 species per year. Experts estimate that 50 species per day — more than 18,000 a year — are disappearing now. Most of the species lost are plants and insects, but they play an important role in the structure of ecosystems. The Brundtland Commission called the extinctions "the greatest setback to life's abundance and diversity since life first emerged over 3.5 billion years ago." In addition to losing wild species, we are reducing genetic diversity in crops. In India, as many as 30,000 rice varieties existed in late 1970s, but there are estimates that only a dozen will dominate in the 1990s.

World Wildlife Fund Canada says this country has 230 species of mammals, birds, fish and plants that are extinct, extirpated, endangered or threatened. (Extirpated means eliminated in the region or nation, but still living somewhere else in the world.) The passenger pigeon, sea mink and Dawson caribou are gone forever. A host of other plants and animals are facing the slide into oblivion, including the beluga whale of the St. Lawrence estuary, Acadian whitefish, Eskimo curlew and Eastern cougar.

There are ethical questions as to whether we have a right to destroy other forms of life, and there are fundamental questions of self-interest. Our food supply and many medicines are based upon wild species, and we depend upon them for periodic injections of strong genetic material. If we destroy wild plants and animals we reduce our food and medical security. Medicines from the wild are worth about $40 billion a year. More than 5,000 wild species are known to yield chemicals with cancer-fighting potential.

There is another side to the changing species story — the introduction of foreign species. Since 1810, 134 foreign species of life have been introduced into the Great Lakes. The eel-like sea lamprey apparently used shipping canals to bypass the natural barrier of Niagara Falls and devastate upper lakes fisheries. More recently, the zebra mussel hitch-hiked its way across the ocean in the ballast water of a freighter and is now invading parts of the lakes. Each invasion displaces native species and leads to millions of dollars in control measures.

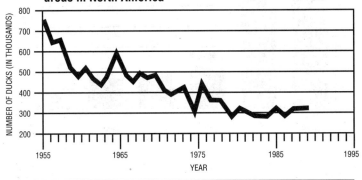

Trend in the numbers of American black ducks in wintering areas in North America

Reproduced with permission from:
Government of Canada, *The State of Canada's Environment — 1991*, Ottawa, 1991.

SPECIAL ISSUES

Energy

The Brundtland Report says: "The ultimate limits to global development are perhaps determined by the availability of energy resources and by the biosphere's capacity to absorb the by-products of energy use."

Canada's per capita energy use is the highest in the world, and Canadians obtain three quarters of their primary energy from fossil fuels: oil, natural gas and coal. Hydro-electric power and nuclear energy each account for about 10 per cent of Canada's energy supply, and wood provides the remaining 5 per cent. The energy needed to support the average Canadian's lifestyle is equivalent to nearly nine tonnes of oil a year.

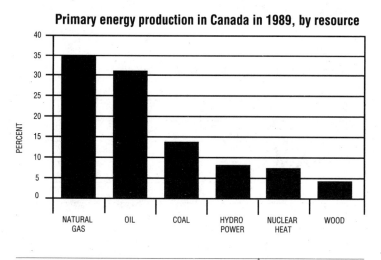

Primary energy production in Canada in 1989, by resource

Reproduced with permission from:
Government of Canada, *The State of Canada's Environment — 1991*, Ottawa, 1991.

Energy use can be more efficient. A process called co-generation can tap huge amounts of energy that are discharged as waste heat by industries. The heat can be used, sold as steam, or harnessed to generate electricity. Alternatives to burning more fossil fuels include solar panels, wind generators, biomass, geothermal, wave power, human and animal power. Small-scale hydro-electric generators tap the power of moving streams without requiring major dams. Wood and other plants can be burned or used to produce fuel alcohol in a process called biomass energy. If trees and crops are re-planted, they remove the carbon dioxide from the air.

In a 1988 report, the federal Energy Options Advisory Committee said that using available technology, "current energy inputs in major energy-using sectors could be profitably lowered by 20 to 30 per cent without reducing the output of products and services." The average American-made car must get 27.5 miles per U.S. gallon of gasoline, and this sets the pace for cars sold in Canada. Cars that get 50 miles per gallon are available, but relatively few are purchased. Cars that get close to 100 miles per gallon have been made in prototype versions, and would be sold if demand existed. We can buy light bulbs that are 80 per cent more energy-efficient than those commonly used, and refrigerators that are twice as efficient. Some high-tech windows are able to capture significant amounts of heat from sunlight.

Nuclear energy, nuclear wastes and radiation

Nuclear power, which provides about 15 per cent of all electricity worldwide and about the same amount in Canada, is praised by its advocates as an energy source that does not produce acid rain and greenhouse gases. However, the nuclear power plant accidents at Three Mile Island in 1979 and Chernobyl in 1986 made many people nervous about this energy source, and the rate of investment in nuclear energy declined sharply in most countries during the 1980s.

In Canada, nuclear power is produced by 16 reactors in Ontario and one each in Quebec and New Brunswick. The Canadian reactors are the Canadian Deuterium-Uranium (CANDU) system. Several of these reactors have had a considerable number of small leaks of mildly radioactive materials, but no major releases. They face high construction costs for safety reasons, high maintenance costs because of unexpected breakdowns, and the costly problem of waste disposal. High-level radioactive wastes can remain dangerous for thousands of years, and fuel bundles from CANDU reactors are now mostly stored in deep pools of water at the reactor sites while research is conducted on long-term storage. The major research centre is at the Whiteshell Laboratories at Pinawa, Manitoba, where a shaft has been drilled into deep granite in an effort to see if the Canadian Shield can provide safe storage. Low-level radioactive wastes are in storage areas or in tailings piles beside uranium mine sites. There are more than 120 million tonnes of low-level radioactive wastes exposed to elements in Canada. (For more information on radiation, see Radiation in the reference section.)

Garbage

For millennia, humans have thrown their wastes into pits in the ground that drew flies, rats and birds and generally stank. In recent years, governments have been calling them landfills, even "sanitary landfills." Even if the garbage is periodically covered with earth to keep down the smell, decaying wastes can escape into the air as gases, or form liquids called leachate, that can seep into underground water supplies. Such leakage can be controlled by lining and eventually covering the pits with plastic and clay. Some landfills are ringed with underground collection pipes to catch leachate, and some have pipes to collect landfill gases. These gases can be burned for energy.

Canadians have the dubious distinction of being the world's greatest garbage producers, throwing out nearly 2 kilograms per person per day. When you add wastes from restaurants, offices, hospitals, stores, factories and construction sites, it adds up to about 30 million tonnes a year. Count other wastes — from mining, dredging, agriculture and heavy industries — and Canada produces more than 200 million tonnes of waste a year. Most municipal garbage goes into 10,000 dumps across the country. People often wonder what is filling up the dumps. Packaging, which makes up about one third of garbage, is the largest single waste category. Most of the packaging is paper and cardboard. Plastic accounts for less than five per cent.

Canada's Residential Waste Stream (by weight)

(Canada's Green Plan, 1990)

Paper and cardboard	36.4 %
Food wastes and decayables	27.6 %
Glass	6.6 %
Metal	6.6 %
Yard waste	6.1 %

Plastics	4.6 %
Textiles	4.3 %
Wood	4.2 %
Other	3.5 %

For years there has been confusion about how fast garbage breaks down in the ground. Excavations, particularly by William Rathje, an archeologist and "garbologist" from the University of Arizona, have provided answers in Canada and the United States. In 1991, a team that included Mr. Rathje excavated material from four Southern Ontario dumps. They found readable newspapers dating from the early 1950s, showing this material is very slow to degrade. Food debris and yard wastes do degrade, but the process is also very slow. Steel cans will degrade into rusting bits over a few decades. The dig also showed that in recent years, when recycling was introduced, there was a decline in the amount of newspapers, glass and cans being dumped. Since the 1950s, the type of packaging being dumped has shifted from heavy glass to thinner glass bottles, paper and light-weight plastic.

What we throw away: the composition of residential waste in Ontario, 1989

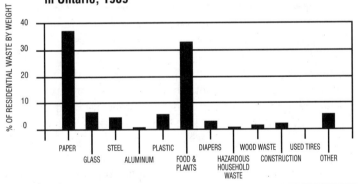

Reproduced with permission from:
Government of Canada, _The State of Canada's Environment — 1991_, Ottawa, 1991.

Incineration is another method of waste disposal. In theory, any organic chemical can be reduced to basic elements such as carbon dioxide, water vapour, salt and metals, if it is heated hot enough and long enough, but in practice, only very sophisticated incinerators designed to burn toxic chemicals can control the release of harmful substances to very small levels. In less-efficient incinerators, harmful by-products such as dioxins, furans and acids are released from chimneys. Metals are not destroyed by incineration, and go up the stacks as fine particles. Much unburned material, such as soot and metal particles, can be captured by well-designed anti-pollution systems, including scrubbers and baghouse filter systems. This results in a toxic residue that is usually landfilled, along with the ash, which also contains toxic heavy metals.

Canadians have started recycling and reducing waste, and this is starting to put a dent in the waste stream. Between 1987 and 1992, the amount of waste going to landfills and incinerators from Ontario's municipal, commercial and institutional sectors fell by 21 per cent. This is non-hazardous solid waste from homes, stores, schools, hospitals, office buildings and factories. The Canadian Council of Ministers of the Environment has set a nationwide goal of reducing the weight of the nation's municipal garbage by 50 per cent by the year 2000. Curbside recycling in Canada usually can take about 15 per cent of household waste, in the form of newspapers, cans and bottles, but it could capture as much as 60 per cent with the addition of other materials, including all types of plastics, paper and cardboard boxes. Further large reductions in garbage can be made by composting food and garden wastes which take up nearly half the garbage in some residential areas.

Even though recycling is often in the news, it is the last of the three Rs cited as the keys to controlling waste. They are: reduction, re-use and recycling. An August 1992 commentary, adapted from the *Warmer Bulletin* from Great Britain, puts the three techniques in this perspective:

"The trouble with recycling is that it clouds the issue. It enables people to believe that they have done something about the waste they generate, to assuage any guilt they might otherwise have felt about their consumption, and gives them tacit permission to continue to live in exactly the same way. Too many people believe that recycling paper, glass or metal answers that need. Sadly, while recycling undoubtedly helps a little, recycling alone is approaching the problem from the wrong end. The first priority on the agreed waste management hierarchy is waste minimization. The next priority is re-using goods, which does actually contribute to reducing overall waste, and with very low additional costs in terms of energy and resources. The best way to manage waste of any kind is simply not to produce it in the first place."

Hazardous waste

The United Nations Environment Programme reports that at least 338 million tonnes of hazardous industrial waste are produced each year, with 275 million tonnes from the United States. However the UN figure does not give a full picture of the world's hazardous waste problem, since there is little reporting of this problem from a number of nations, including most of those in the former Soviet bloc.

Canada produces around 6.5 million tonnes of hazardous industrial wastes per year. In addition, each Canadian disposes of about 2.5 kilograms of household hazardous waste each year, including paint, solvents, batteries, pesticides, cleaners and swimming pool chemicals. Canada has about 1,000 hazardous waste sites that need to be controlled, including coal tar pits, leaking landfills, old factory and storage sites. Each site can cost from several hundred thousand to tens of millions of dollars to clean up, and many must be rehabilitated at public expense, because the original owners have disappeared. In some cases, such as a dump near Mercier, in the Montreal area, leaking chemicals have contaminated the underground water over a wide area, and it is no longer safe to drink.

Note: When covering garbage and industrial waste stories, make certain you know what the figures represent. There is residential waste, from homes, and there is municipal waste, which also includes waste from small stores and offices that use curbside pickup. The term municipal waste sometimes includes the industrial, commercial and institutional (ICI) sector, whose garbage is often removed by private contractors. This includes offices, schools, hospitals and businesses. In the industrial sector there is liquid and solid hazardous and non-hazardous waste. There is also waste such as mine tailings and waste wood. There is waste which is collected and treated on plant sites or off-site by private companies, and there is waste which is discharged onto the land, into the water or the air.

Chemicals

Chemicals are a natural part of the environment. Our bodies are made up of natural chemicals, and so is our food. The chemicals must be in correct balance, or we will get ill or die. Both natural and synthetic chemicals are an essential part of our industrial society. They are used to make clothes, medicines and cars, preserve foods and air condition homes and offices. About 10 million chemical compounds have been synthesized in laboratories. Globally, about 1 per cent — 100,000 organic and inorganic chemicals — are produced commercially, and 1,000 to 2,000 new ones are created each year. About 35,000 of these commercial chemicals are used in Canada, and 100 to 200 new ones are brought onto the Canadian market annually. A number of substances called chemicals are actually metals, including the heavy metals, mercury, lead, cadmium and selenium. There are also non-metallic minerals such as asbestos. Some chemicals in the news have been deliberately made for specific uses, including CFCs, PCBs and DDT. Other chemicals, such as dioxins and furans, are accidental waste by-products of some industrial processes and the burning of some chemical mixtures.

Synthetic organic chemicals

Most stories about toxic chemicals involve synthetic organic (contains carbon) chemicals. They are usually made from a combination of petroleum and halogens, such as chlorine, bromine and, to a lesser extent, fluorine and iodine. Chlorine is the most common of the halogens encountered in environmental stories. Compounds made with chlorine are variously called organochlorines, chlorinated organics or simply OCs. Organochlorine molecules also contain atoms of hydrogen and oxygen. Because petroleum is a hydrocarbon (it contains hydrogen and carbon) these chemicals are also called halogenated hydrocarbons or organohalogens. These chemicals form the basis of a wide range of materials, including plastics and pesticides. The molecules are made and modified by adding chlorine gas to petroleum products under different combinations of heat, pressure and time. This class of chemicals tends to be persistent, meaning they do not break down easily in the environment. A number of them also accumulate in fat cells of living organisms.

Chlorine is also used by itself by industries, municipalities and households. It bleaches pulp, thus making paper whiter. In municipalities, chlorine is used to disinfect drinking water and sewage by killing harmful microbes. At home, chlorine is used in many bleaches to whiten clothes.

Pesticides

Pesticides have been used to get rid of unwanted plants and animals as far back as 2500 BC, when sulphur was used to kill insects. Since the late 1940s, there has been an explosion in the number of synthetic organic chemical pesticides. Now there are five main classes: insecticides, herbicides, fungicides, rodenticides, and miscellaneous pesticides such as repellents, hormone growth regulators, preservatives, soaps and oils. The toxicity of pesticides to humans and wildlife ranges from very low, in the cases of substances such as soaps, to very high in the case of chemicals which can attack the nervous system of mammals.

For years, there has been a steady arrival of new pesticides on the market. One of the reasons is pesticide resistance in insects. A few insects that have a natural resistance to each pesticide survive, and they are the ones that breed. This means that pesticide-resistant strains of insects develop, and new chemicals are created in response. Agriculture Canada has registered more than 500 active chemical ingredients for pesticides, and about 100 are used regularly in a wide variety of formulations.

The first major organochlorine insecticide was DDT, which disrupts the nervous systems of insects. Developed in the 1940s, it launched modern pest control with widespread spray programs. DDT, which is very harmful to wildlife, has been banned in Canada and a number of countries, but is still widely used in many tropical nations, particularly to kill disease-bearing mosquitoes. Since the mid-1970s, many organochlorine insecticides have been replaced in Canada with less persistent chemicals.

The most widely used group of insecticides in the world is the organophospate family, a mix of petroleum products and phosphoric acid. It includes such chemicals as parathion, malathion, chlorpyrifos and diazinon. Organophosphates, related to nerve gas, interfere with enzymes in the nervous system, and they can be hazardous to humans if handled carelessly. Organophosphates tend to break down into elements such as phosphoric acid when in contact with water and are less likely to accumulate in living creatures than organochlorines. Carbamates, a third class of insecticides, are relatively selective and behave in many ways like organophosphates. They tend not to build up in the food chain. Aldicarb, a carbamate, is the most acutely toxic pesticide registered for use in Canada. Other types of insecticides include pyrethrum, derived from a flower, finely-ground seashells, sulphur and insecticidal soaps.

A wide range of chemicals are used as herbicides — substances that kill plants. One of the best known is 2,4-D, a phenoxy herbicide which was brought into use in the 1940s. It has been used for everything from killing dandelions on lawns to defoliating jungles during wartime.

What is a toxic substance?

The 1978 Great Lakes Water Quality Agreement defines a toxic substance as:
> "a substance which can cause death, disease, behavioral abnormalities, cancer, genetic mutations, physiological or reproductive malfunctions or physical deformities in any organism or its offspring, or which can become poisonous after

concentration in the food chain or in combination with other substances."

A number of toxic materials are tasteless, colourless and odourless, particularly in the concentrations usually found in the environment. They can only be detected by sophisticated equipment, and each test can cost hundreds of dollars. There are two general categories of toxicity. Acute toxicity refers to severe harm or death in a short period of time. Chronic or sub-lethal toxicity refers to harm that takes place after long-term exposure. It involves diseases such as cancers, which can take decades to develop.

Some hazardous materials break down within hours or days in the environment when exposed to sunlight or water. Other chemicals, such as PCBs, are very persistent and resistant to natural breakdown. One definition of a persistent chemical is that it will not degrade to at least half its original quantity within eight weeks in the natural environment. Some harmful materials are natural phenomena that become toxic through human action. Radon gas is naturally released from some soils, but is trapped in basements and uranium mines, and breathing it can be harmful. Heavy metals, asbestos and radionuclides become toxic when extracted from the earth, concentrated and released into the environment in ways that can cause environmental damage or health problems.

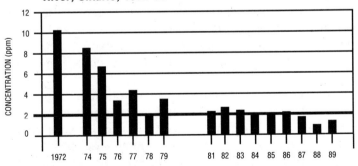

Mean concentrations of PCBs in coho salmon from the Credit River, Ontario, 1972-89

2.0 ppm= federal guideline for unrestricted consumption.

Reproduced with permission from:
Government of Canada, *The State of Canada's Environment — 1991*, Ottawa, 1991.

Controlling harmful substances

Canada has banned or strictly controlled such hazardous substances as dioxins, furans, DDT, PCBs, mercury, lead, mirex and chlordane. These include products that were deliberately manufactured, such as pesticides, and accidental by-products of manufacture, such as dioxins. Environment Canada is to complete toxicity assessments of 44 chemicals by 1994 and 100 by the year 2000, under the Canadian Environmental Protection Act. Canada's National Pollutants Release Inventory (NPRI) will identify sources of major pollutants from industry and will provide estimates on how much of each pollutant is released. The first report will be made public in 1994. Contact public affairs officers in Environment Canada for further information. (See contact list later in this handbook.)

In 1992, Ontario's Environment Ministry released a list of 21 hazardous substances for possible ban or phase-out in the province. These chemicals are in the environment, and are considered hazardous because of three criteria: persistence, bioaccumulation potential and toxicity. The ministry has a secondary list of 46 substances that are toxic and either persistent or build up in the food chain.

In 1991, the New Directions Group issued recommendations for reducing and eliminating the emission of toxic substances. The New Directions Group is composed of 21 people, mainly leaders from industry and environmental organizations. The group called on the federal government to develop a national emissions inventory for toxic substances and the sunsetting (phase out and ban) of certain hazardous substances. It suggested starting with the 11 critical pollutants identified by the International Joint Commission.

Since the mid-1980s, the Canadian Chemical Producers' Association (CCPA) has been implementing a program called Responsible Care. It requires the 70 CCPA member companies to ensure that their operations do not present an unacceptable risk to people or the environment, to make chemical hazard information available to the public, and to help people understand how to use chemicals safely. In 1990, the Responsible Care program won a

Global 500 award from the United Nations Environment Programme. *The State of Canada's Environment* report says that some chemical companies will not supply chemicals to customers that do not meet standards for safe operations. CCPA is establishing a National Emissions Reduction Masterplan (NERM). CCPA members will be required to report their emissions to CCPA, from a list of more than 300 toxic and non-toxic substances of health and environmental concern. By the latter part of 1993, CCPA plans to voluntarily start releasing annual reports on emissions.

Harmful substances in the news

The following is a list of a number of harmful chemicals and metals that periodically turn up in the news. The list is not exhaustive and the descriptions are basic outlines.

Eleven Critical Pollutants

(from the list of the Great Lakes Water Quality Board of the International Joint Commission, adopted by the New Directions Group)

- PCBs (industrial chemicals)
- DDT and its breakdown products (pesticide)
- dieldrin (pesticide)
- toxaphene (pesticide)
- dioxin (2,3,7,8-TCDD) (waste by-product)
- furan (2,3,7,8-TCDF) (waste by-product)
- mirex (pesticide, industrial chemical)
- mercury (industrial metal)
- benzo(a)pyrene (waste by-product)
- hexachlorobenzene (pesticide, by-product)
- alkylated lead (industrial compound and former gasoline additive)

- *PCBs (polychlorinated biphenyls)* — This is a family of chemicals with 209 possible variations. Some members of this family have similar chemical structures and bio-chemical characteristics to dioxins. Since the 1930s, PCBs have been used widely in electrical, hydraulic and other equipment, and until the 1970s they were used in such consumer products as home fluorescent lights, paints and carbonless copy paper. PCBs are no longer made or sold in North America, but they still used in thousands of older pieces of electrical equipment such as transformers. PCBs periodically escape into the environment in spills, or when old equipment is junked. PCBs are widely dispersed in the environment, are very persistent and accumulate dramatically in the food chain. They cause cancer in laboratory animal tests, and have been linked to health problems such as embryo mortality and deformities in wildlife. Sustained, high-level exposure to PCBs has been associated with such human health effects as a severe form of acne (chloracne), eye discharge, swelling of eyelids, numbness of limbs, muscle spasms, chronic bronchitis, and decreased birth weight and head circumference in newborns. Health and Welfare Canada states that short-term, low-level exposure to PCBs is unlikely to have significant health impacts, but there is concern over long-term exposure to low levels. Studies have found an association between prenatal exposure to PCBs and slight reductions in mental development. There is limited evidence that long-term exposure to high PCB levels may cause cancer in humans, particularly liver cancer, and PCBs are listed as probably cancer-causing to humans. (See section on Environment and Health.)

• *DDT and its metabolites (breakdown products in the environment), particularly DDE* — The full chemical name for DDT is dichlorodiphenyltrichloroethane. The insecticide was first widely used after the Second World War, but was restricted in Canada and the United States starting in the 1960s, and is now banned. In insects, DDT disrupts the body's chemical system of hormones and enzymes. There is no clear evidence of serious health effects on people, but DDT is listed as possibly cancer-causing to humans. There is plenty of evidence that the pesticide has caused considerable harm to wildlife, including eggshell thinning in a number of fish-eating birds, mortality of embryos, and sterility in wildlife, especially birds. In recent years, it has been associated with sex changes in embryos. DDT still enters the Canadian environment, probably from a combination of sources. These include long-range airborne transport from countries where it is used, leakage from some Canadian chemical dumps, and possibly from the illegal use of old stocks.

48

- *Dieldrin and the related pesticide, aldrin* — These persistent chemicals were used mainly as insecticides, starting in 1948. Both are manufactured chemicals, but aldrin is also naturally degraded to dieldrin in the environment. Dieldrin has been linked to the death of adult bald eagles in the Great Lakes basin. Dieldrin levels in herring gull eggs and fish in several areas sampled in the Great Lakes have not declined since mid-1970s. Dieldrin is still used for termite control.

- *Toxaphene* — This chemical, chemically similar to DDT, was once the most heavily used insecticide in the United States, and was applied extensively to cotton crops in the U.S. southeast. Large amounts of it blew north to land on the Great Lakes, building up to substantial levels in fish in Lake Superior, and toxaphene has been detected in wildlife as far north as the Arctic. The use of toxaphene is now restricted in the United States, and there are minimal registrations in Canada.

- *Dioxins* — This is a family of 75 chlorinated chemicals, which vary greatly in toxicity. The family is known as polychlorinated dibenzo dioxins or PCDDs. The 2,3,7,8-TCDD variant is considered the most toxic synthetic chemical known. Its full name is 2,3, 7,8-tetrachlorodibenzo-para-dioxin. Dioxins are not made deliberately, but are unwanted by-products of combustion and some industrial processes that use chlorine. Dioxins come from a wide variety of other sources, including incinerators and the chlorine bleaching of pulp and paper. The 2,3,7,8-TCDD isomer is highly toxic to many animals in minuscule doses, and is believed responsible for an outbreak of the fatal chick edema disease in Lake Ontario herring gulls in 1970s. Dioxins cause death, birth defects, cancer, immune system problems, disruptions in cell growth and a wasting syndrome in laboratory animals, depending on the dose. High levels cause damage to the central nervous system and to a number of human organs, including the liver and heart. The effects of low levels of dioxins on humans are not well understood, but dioxins are considered a hazardous class of chemicals and 2,3,7,8-TCDD is listed as possibly cancer-causing to humans.

- *Furans* — This family of chlorinated chemicals has 135 variations or isomers. The technical name is polychlorinated dibenzo furans or

PCDFs. Like dioxins, furans are accidental wastes and are by-products of the manufacture of chlorophenol chemicals, and the same processes that produce dioxins. The 2,3,7,8-TCDF variant is similar in chemical structure to TCDD dioxin, but is about one quarter as toxic. Furans are often found as contaminants in PCBs.

• *Benzo(a)pyrene (B(a)P)* — This is a member of polynuclear aromatic hydrocarbons (PAH) family of chemicals. PAHs are a waste by-product of the incomplete combustion of fossil fuels and wood, incineration, steel and coke production, and coal liquefaction and gasification. B(a)P is listed as probably cancer-causing to humans. In the case of humans, the major exposure has been through inhalation at workplaces. PAHs have also been associated with cancers in fish in highly contaminated areas around some old steel works. When PAHs have been applied to the skin of test fish, tumors developed.

• *Hexachlorobenzene* — This chemical was used as a fungicide for cereal crops, and it is also a contaminant or by-product of the making of some other pesticides. HCB is persistent, and is found in the tissues of fish, animals and humans in regions such as the Great Lakes basin. It interferes with enzymes that control the production of hemoglobin, a constituent of blood. In tests, HCB affects the nerves and causes liver damage, reproductive effects and cancer in laboratory animals. Excessive hexachlorobenzene doses have caused death among infants. Limited uses of HCB are still permitted in Canada.

• *Mirex* — Mirex is an extremely persistent chemical that was used as a fire retardant and a pesticide. It was once packaged along the Niagara River and the shore of Lake Ontario, and is found in that lake and downstream into the St. Lawrence River. In laboratory animals, Mirex causes reproductive problems and cancer, and it is listed as possibly cancer-causing to humans. Mirex was banned from import to Canada in 1978. Its main use as a pesticide was to kill fire ants in the southern United States.

• *Mercury* — This is an industrial metal that has a very wide variety of uses, ranging from thermometers to the manufacture of chlorine and caustic soda. Mercury use has been controlled in some industrial processes and pesticides. The metal is still used in consumer products, including some street lamps, paints, batteries and light switches, and can be released into the environment when these are discarded. Mercury vapor is also released by the burning of fuels containing traces of mercury, particularly coal. Mercury can build up in the brain, kidney and liver, and harm the human nervous system. A number of fisheries have closed since 1970 because of mercury pollution.

• *Lead* — For decades, alkyl lead, particularly tetraethyl lead, was added to gasoline to boost its performance. Lead has been virtually banned from use in Canadian motor fuel, with only very small amounts allowed in fuel for certain engines. Ordinary metallic lead is still used in such products as automotive batteries. Like mercury, lead is a neurotoxin. Studies show that quite small amounts of lead can cause irreversible brain damage to infants and young children. Lead has also been found in the environment around smelting plants, and in atmospheric fallout across a wide area.

Some other harmful substances in the news

• *Trichlorethylene* — This chemical has been widely used to remove grease from metal parts. Used trichlorethylene has been dumped in landfills, from which it has seeped into underground water sources, and contaminated a number of wells.

• *Perchloroethylene* — Also called tetrachloroethylene, it has long been used as dry cleaning fluid, although this use is diminishing in Canada. It can be hazardous when breathed in large quantities, causes cancer in test animals, and is considered possibly cancer causing to humans.

• *Pentachlorophenol* — Widely used as wood preservative since 1930s, it is now being phased out of this use. It is sometimes found in dumps or in the ground around wood preserving operations, and often contains dioxins and furans as impurities. In humans, pentachlorophenol can cause a range of effects from skin irritation to weight loss, liver and kidney damage.

• *Trihalomethanes* — Known as THMs, these chemicals are formed when chlorine comes in contact with organic compounds, including natural organic matter in the water. THMs are produced by the chlorination of drinking water and sewage. THMs include chloroform, bromo-dichloromethane, chlorodibromomethane and bromoform. Chloroform is a proven carcinogen in animals, and a possible carcinogen in humans.

The Canadian Environmental Protection Act
Priority Substances List as of 1992

Chemicals are being evaluated for control, based on the following criteria:

• Causes or has potential to cause adverse effects on human health or the environment.
• Accumulates or could accumulate to significant concentrations in air, water, soil, sediment or tissue.
• Is released into the environment in significant quantities or concentrations.

The substances scheduled for earliest assessment are:

• arsenic and its compounds
• benzene
• effluents from pulp mills using bleaching
• hexachlorobenzene
• methyl tertiary-butyl ether
• polychlorinated dibenzodioxins
• polychlorinated dibenzofurans
• polycyclic aromatic hydrocarbons
• waste crankcase oils

(Pulp mill effluent and waste crankcase oils from motor vehicles are families of chemicals, each containing several hundred members of varying toxicity.)

The 1992 list of 21 hazardous substances for possible ban or phase-out in Ontario

- anthracene
- arsenic
- benzo(a)pyrene
- benzo(ghi)perylene
- benz(a)anthracene
- DDT (including DDD and DDE)
- 1,4-dichlorobenzene
- 3,3-dichlorobenzidene
- dieldrin
- hexachlorobenzene
- alpha-1,2,3,4,5,6-hexachorocyclohexane
- gamma-1,2,3,4,5,6-hexachorocyclohexane (Lindane)
- mercury
- mirex
- pentachlorophenol
- perylene
- phenanthrene
- polychlorinated biphenyls (PCBs)
- polychlorinated dibenzo-p-dioxins and -furans
- toxaphene
- tributyl tin

Note: There are some obvious and not so obvious overlaps in lists. For example, the federal list refers to polycyclic aromatic hydrocarbons (PAHs). The Ontario list refers to benzo(a)pyrene B(a)P, one of the PAHs. In the case of DDT, the substance is already banned.

ENVIRONMENT AND HEALTH

"Health is a state of complete physical, mental and social well-being, and not merely the absence of disease or infirmity." — World Health Organization.

Humans have been creating environmental health problems ever since they started building fires in caves, then breathed in the smoke. The term "mad as a hatter" evolved centuries ago, referring to people who used mercury in the making of felt hats. Toxic chemicals and metals can have a wide range of harmful effects. The effect depends upon the dose. In some cases, there is no known effect if the dose is small enough. For substances that cause cancer, researchers are not certain if there is a dose small enough to have no effect.

Among the terms you will encounter:

- *Carcinogenic* means it initiates or promotes the development of cancer. (Some substances can initiate a cancer by themselves, but others can only promote the formation of a tumor by another substance.)

- *Teratogenicity* means that it causes birth defects.

- *Fetotoxicity* means that it causes death of a fetus.

- *Mutagenicity* means that it causes mutations in cells that can be passed from one generation to another.

- *Neurological* disorders mean that the nervous system is affected.

- *Immunosuppression* means that the substance interferes with the immune system that protects living creatures from illness.

Toxic chemical effects recorded in wildlife include: cancer, death, eggshell thinning, population declines, reduced hatching success, abnormal behaviour such as abandonment of nests, infertility, birth defects such as crossed beaks and club feet, and illnesses such as chick edema. Edema refers to the accumulation of fluid in body cavities. There are also less visible effects on body chemistry, including abnormalities in the thyroid, liver and endocrine systems. DDT causes eggshell thinning by inhibiting the action of enzymes that cause the laying down of calcium to form the shells. The resulting eggs are so thin that they break when the parents try to incubate them.

Some organochlorines appear to have the ability to mimic or block the normal functioning of hormones, and this interferes with natural body processes. It takes only a few molecules of a substance such as PCBs during the development of a fetus to replace a natural hormone in a cell structure, and cause a birth defect. Researchers believe that some organochlorines, such as DDT, may be changing the sexual development of some wildlife. They say that when DDT has been injected into gull eggs, it caused changed the sex of the embryos.

The effects of toxic chemicals on humans are less well understood because we must rely on studies based on accidental exposure. From such cases we know that mercury can cause nervous system damage and death. We know that some chemicals cause human cancers and a number of other illnesses to the skin, nervous system and organs. Scientists are now turning up signs of more subtle effects from relatively low levels of some persistent toxic chemicals. The children of mothers who ate an average of 6.7 kilograms (15 pounds) of contaminated fish a year from Lake Michigan were born earlier, weighed less and had smaller head sizes than the children of non fish eaters. The children of fish eaters were also more easily startled, had abnormally weak reflexes and were less able to detect differences in visual images in front of them. At age four, these children had poorer verbal skills and poorer short-term memories than normal youngsters, based on psychological testing. Researchers feel the adverse effects were most likely caused by chemicals, possibly PCBs, passed from the mother to the fetus through the placenta.

Reporting on health risks from hazardous substances is often very frustrating, because of the lack of clear information. Risk estimates are based upon knowing the exposure, but in the case of contaminants which turn up on food or in the air or water, it is often impossible to know the true dose. Then there is often a lack of clear toxicological information. According to the United States National Research Council, there is sufficient information to allow a complete health hazard assessment for less than two per cent of commercially produced chemicals. For another 14 per cent, there is enough information for a partial hazard assessment.

Canada regulates public exposure to chemical residues under the Food and Drug Act. The *Guidelines for Canadian Drinking Water*

Quality set acceptable levels for a number of substances in drinking water.

Cancer causing substances

One of the most authoritative sources of information on cancer causing materials is the International Agency for Research on Cancer (IARC), an arm of the World Health Organization. The following list is drawn from an IARC publication. Not all cancer causing agents on the IARC list are listed here, because some are not likely to turn up in environmental stories. IARC lists individual substances and some industrial processes with a cancer risk.

Group 1

Some agents that are known to be carcinogenic (cancer causing) to humans

Aflatoxins
Aluminium production
Arsenic
Asbestos
Benzene
Chromium compounds, hexavalent (not all of them)
Coal gasification, coal tars and coal tar pitches
Coke production
Iron and steel founding
Nickel and nickel compounds (not all of them)
Rubber industry
Shale oils
Soots
Tobacco products and tobacco smoke
Vinyl chloride

Group 2A

Some agents that are probably carcinogenic (cancer causing) to humans

Benz(a)anthracene
Benzo(a)pyrene
Cadmium and cadmium compounds
Creosotes
Dimethyl sulphate

Ethylene dibromide
Ethylene oxide
Formaldehyde
Polychlorinated biphenyls (PCBs)
Propylene oxide
Styrene oxide
Vinyl oxide

Group 2B

Some agents that are possibly carcinogenic (cancer causing) to humans

Benzo(b)fluoranthene
Benzo(j)fluoranthene
Benzo(k)fluoranthene
Bitumens (extracts of steam-refined and air-refined)
1,3-Butadiene
Carbon-black extracts
Carbon tetrachloride
Chlordecone (Kepone)
Chlorinated toluenes
Chloroform
Chlorophenols
Chlorophenoxy herbicides
DDT
para-Dichlorobenzene
1,2-Dichloroethane
Dichloromethane
Hexachlorobenzene
Hexachlorocyclohexanes
Lead and lead compounds, inorganic
Mirex
Polybrominated biphenyls (PBBs)
Saccharin
Styrene
2,3,7,8-tetrachlorodibenzo-para-dioxin (TCDD)
Tetrachloroethylene
Toxaphene
Urethane

Bioaccumulation and bioconcentration

"The adipose (fatty) tissue of all Canadians has become a rich repository of fat-soluble environmental contaminants, including large numbers of pesticides, flame retardants and industrial transformer fluids."— Ecotoxicity: Responsibilities and Opportunities, by Ross H. Hall and Donald A. Chant.

The environmental hazard of a toxic substance cannot always be judged by the volume discharged. Some of the most worrisome chemicals are those that do not break down in the environment, and build up in the food chain. This means that relatively small amounts can eventually have serious effects. There are two important processes in the passage of persistent toxic chemicals through the food chain:

Bioaccumulation takes place when toxic substances are absorbed and retained by living creatures. The substances can be taken in directly from the environment, or can be consumed along with food. Organochlorine chemicals are highly soluble in fat, so they accumulate in fatty cells and remain in living organisms.

Biomagnification is the process of passing increasing levels of toxic substances up the food chain, when the rate of intake is greater than the rate at which they are excreted or metabolized. PCB levels in the blubber of marine mammals that live in the Arctic Ocean are up to 400 million times higher than levels in the water.

Bioaccumulation and biomagnification of PCBs in the Great Lakes aquatic food chain

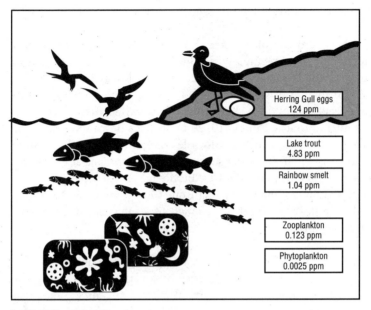

| Herring Gull eggs |
| 124 ppm |

Lake trout
4.83 ppm

Rainbow smelt
1.04 ppm

Zooplankton
0.123 ppm

Phytoplankton
0.0025 ppm

Reproduced with permission from:
Government of Canada, *The State of Canada's Environment — 1991*, Ottawa, 1991.

Risk and risk assessment

"All things are poisons, for there is nothing without poisonous qualities. It is only the dose which makes a thing a poison."
— Paracelsus, Sixteenth Century Swiss physician and philosopher.

Advice on what is an acceptable limit of a given substance in our food, air and water is based on a complex but little-known procedure called risk assessment. In a few tragic cases, we have direct knowledge about how much of a certain substance it takes to poison people. Mainly, we have to rely on the results of tests on laboratory animals, which are then used to predict the effects on humans. The test animals, usually rats, mice or guinea pigs, are fed decreasing doses of a suspect poison in search of two key pieces of information. The first, the LD50 or lethal dose which will kill 50 per cent of the animals outright, gives a relative degree of immediate danger from the substance. The second is the level at which there are no observed adverse effects over a tests of several weeks or months. This level is variously referred to as No Observed Effects Level (NOEL) and No Observed Adverse Effects Level (NOAEL).

The guardians of our health are still left with two difficult questions. How accurately do the tests on animals translate to humans, who have a different metabolism, and may be more or less resistant to a given substance? And how do you deal with the fact that effects too subtle to show up in relatively short-term laboratory tests might produce cancers 10, 20 or 30 years down the road? The experts try to predict a "virtually safe dosage" by extrapolating from the decreasing effects of the substance on test animals at ever lower dosages. They will take the NOAEL dosage as a starting point, and divide that by a number, ranging from 10 to as much as 10,000, to produce a dose they feel has enough of a safety factor to protect human health.

Another way of determining risk is through epidemiology— the study of effects of a given substance on a certain population. The researcher attempts to find a harmful effect that can be linked to a specific cause. This technique works best when a group is known to have been exposed to a relatively high dose of a specific substance. In real life this technique is often imprecise, because people are exposed to varying doses of a number of toxic substances. It is often difficult to tell which substance caused the harm, or if the damage was caused by other factors, such as a damaged gene.

The State of Canada's Environment says that: "For carcinogenic substances and ionizing radiation, there is evidence that there is no level of exposure at which a hazard does not exist. Guidelines are set at levels at which the risk is thought to be sufficiently low or negligible, i.e., one person in a million developing cancer." That means that out of one million people exposed to the same level of a substance on a daily basis, only one would be predicted to suffer adverse effects during a normal lifetime. (One in one million is frequently used as a guideline because it is about the same risk as being struck by lightning.) Technical documents sometimes show risk estimates in such forms as 1 in 10^{-6} which means one in one million.

Concept of exposure

A common weakness in pollution stories is the failure to explain adequately the potential for harm from an environmental contaminant. Too often the story says something like: "A cancer causing chemical was released into the environment today, but officials said there is no risk." What kind of a message does that give? Potential risk only becomes real risk when there is exposure and when the dose is high enough to have an effect. In each story that suggests there may be risk, the journalist should provide information about possible routes of exposure and how much exposure is likely needed to cause harm.

Routes of exposure include breathing, drinking, absorption through the skin or across the placenta to a fetus, and in mothers' milk. The most vulnerable stage in life is the fetal level, when the body is being formed. Infants and children are also much more vulnerable to toxic substances, because their immune systems are not fully developed. As well, children eat much more food relative to their body weight than do adults. It is important to ask if officially acceptable levels of contamination in food or drink are based on the consumption and the immune system of an adult or a child.

How pollution controls are set

It is a cornerstone of environmental regulation that it is alright to pollute up to a certain level, and very few laws require zero discharge of a given substance. Regulators go through complex calculations of human health, environmental and economic impacts, seeking a quantity of discharge that is considered "acceptable." This is based on what experts estimate is the capacity of the natural environment to assimilate our pollution without damage that we consider unacceptable. In simple terms, the phrase is "the solution to pollution is dilution." In some cases, the pollution can be absorbed by natural systems without causing major disruptions, but too much dumping, even of "natural" materials, can overwhelm the assimilative capacity of the environment. In the case of persistent toxic chemicals, the dilution principle works in reverse, particularly in water. Persistent materials are concentrated by the food chain, and can build up to levels that have toxic effects.

Another factor in the setting of controls is their cost. It is a rough rule of thumb that control of 80 to 90 per cent of an uncontrolled discharge can be achieved at relatively low cost. Controlling the next 5 to 10 per cent is very costly. The last few per cent are so costly as to be almost prohibitive, using control devices. The alternative is to stop using or producing the harmful substance, or to develop a closed loop system that is virtually leak-proof.

Guidelines for Canadian drinking water quality

The provinces set guidelines or laws governing drinking water in their jurisdiction, while the federal government provides technical advice. The federal government regulates drinking water on lands under its jurisdiction, such as the territories and Indian lands.

The booklet, *Guidelines for Canadian Drinking Water Quality — Fourth Edition, 1989*, is a very useful guidebook on risk levels from a number of toxic substances. It is available from bookstores that carry federal publications, or from the Canadian Government Publishing Centre, Supply and Services Canada, Ottawa, Ontario K1A 0S9. Further information on toxic chemicals and drinking water is available from provincial, territorial and federal environment and health departments.

The following is the list of guidelines for acceptable levels of substances in drinking water, taken from the latest (1989) version of *Guidelines for Canadian Drinking Water Quality*. These guidelines were developed by the Federal-Provincial Subcommittee on Drinking Water, which is composed of members from all provincial and territorial governments, as well as a member from Health and Welfare Canada.

Terms Used

MAC— Maximum Acceptable Concentration of a substance in drinking water every day over a lifetime of consumption. According to the guidelines booklet: "Short-term excursions above the maximum acceptable concentrations do not necessarily mean that the water constitutes an undue risk to health. The amount by which, and the period for which, the maximum acceptable concentration can be exceeded without posing a health risk must be assessed by taking into account the toxicity of the substance involved."

IMAC— Interim Maximum Acceptable Concentration. These levels are set where the federal and provincial health experts do not have enough material to set a MAC.

AO— Aesthetic Objectives. These relate to such issues as taste and odor, rather than to health risks.

The figures in the following table are given are in milligrams per litre (parts per million), except for pH (acidity), colour, taste, odour, temperature and turbidity. A figure such as 5.0 is 5 parts per million, while 0.005 is 5 parts per billion and 0.0005 is 500 parts per trillion.

Most of the figures can be read as parts per billion. For example, the MAC for Aldicarb is 0.009 ppm which equals 9 ppb. The lowest maximum acceptable concentration on the list is for Benzo(a)pyrene at 0.00001 parts per million, which is 10 parts per trillion.

The symbol ≤ stands for the words "at or less than."

Most of the substances listed in the following table are insecticides and herbicides (DDT and 2,4-D) or industrial chemicals. No figures are given for some substances, such as aluminium, dioxins, furans and PCBs. The 1989 guidelines booklet states these are under review and may added in the future.

Summary Table

Parameter	MAC	IMAC	AO	Status
Aldicarb	0.009			
Aldrin + Dieldrin	0.0007			Under Review
Ammonia(1)				Proposed
Arsenic	0.05			Under Review
Asbestos(1)				
Atrazine		0.06		
Azinphos-methyl	0.02			
Barium		1.0		Proposed
Bendiocarb	0.04			
Benzene	0.005			
Benzo(a)pyrene	0.00001			
Boron	5.0			Under Review
Bromoxynil		0.005		
Cadmium	0.005			
Calcium(1)				Proposed
Carbaryl	0.09			
Carbofuran	0.09			
Carbon tetrachloride	0.005			
Chlordane	0.007			Under Review
Chloride			≤250	Proposed
Chlorpyrifos	0.09			
Chromium	0.05			
Color			≤15 TCU	
Copper			≤1.0	Under Review
Cyanazine		0.01		
Cyanide	0.2			Under Review
Diazinon	0.02			
Dicamba	0.12			
Dichlorobenzene, 1,2-	0.2		≤0.003	
Dichlorobenzene, 1,4-	0.005		≤0.001	
DDT and metabolites	0.03			Under Review
Dichloroethane, 1,2-		0.005		Proposed
Dichloromethane	0.05			
Dichlorophenol, 2,4-	0.9		≤0.0003	
2,4-D	0.1			Under Review
Diclofop-methyl	0.009			
Dimethoate		0.02		
Diquat	0.07			
Diuron	0.15			

Parameter	MAC	IMAC	AO	Status
Ethylbenzene			≤0.0024	
Fluoride(2)	1.5			Under Review
Gasoline(1)				
Glyphosate		0.28		
Hardness(3)				
Heptachlor + heptachlor epoxide	0.003			Under Review
Iron			≤0.3	Proposed
Lead(4)	0.01			Proposed
Lindane	0.004			Under Review
Magnesium(1)				Proposed
Malathion	0.19			
Manganese			≤0.05	Proposed
Mercury	0.001			
Methoxychlor	0.9			
Metolachlor		0.05		
Metribuzin	0.08			
Monochlorobenzene	0.08		≤0.03	Proposed
Nitrate(5)	45.0			Proposed
Nitrilotriacetic acid (NTA)	0.05			Under Review
Odor			Inoffensive	
Paraquat		0.01		
Parathion	0.05			
Pentachlorophenol	0.06		≤0.03	
pH (acidity)(6)			6.5-8.5	
Phorate		0.002		
Picloram		0.19		Proposed
Selenium	0.01			
Simazine		0.01		
Sodium(7)			≤200	Proposed
Sulphate(8)			≤500	Proposed
Sulphide (as H2S)			≤0.05	Proposed
Taste			Inoffensive	
Temephos		0.28		
Temperature			≤15°C	
Terbufos		0.001		
Tetrachlorophenol, 2,3,4,6-	0.1		≤0.001	
Toluene			≤0.024	
Total Dissolved Solids			≤500	Under Review
Triallate	0.23			
Trichloroethylene	0.05			Proposed

Parameter	MAC	IMAC	AO	Status
Trichlorophenol, 2,4,6	0.005		≤0.002	
2,4,5-T	0.28		≤0.02	
Trifluralin		0.045		Proposed
Trihalomethanes	0.35			Under Review
Turbidity(9, 10)	1 NTU		≤5 NTU	
Uranium	0.1			
Xylenes			≤0.3	
Zinc			≤5.0	Proposed

Notes

1. Assessment of data indicates no need to set a numerical guideline.

2. Optimum level of fluoride for control of dental decay is 1.0 to 1.2 parts per million.

3. Public acceptance of hardness varies, and the maximum level normally considered acceptable is 500 parts per million. Where water is softened by sodium-ion exchange, it is recommended that a separate, unsoftened supply be used for drinking and cooking.

4. Lead may get into tap water from plumbing systems, so the first water drawn from a tap, especially if has not been run for several hours, should not be used for drinking or cooking.

5. Equivalent to 10.0 parts per million nitrate as nitrogen. Nitrite should not exceed 4.5 parts per million or 1.0 parts per million as nitrogen.

6. Refers to pH scale of acidity (see acid rain section for explanation of pH scale).

7. Some people may want to control sodium levels in their diets.
8. If sulphate exceeds 500 parts per million, it may have a laxative effect.

9. & 10. NTU refers to tubidity (solid particles). Bacteria and viruses may be carried by tiny particles.

Guidelines for disease-causing micro-organisms

1. No sample should contain more than 10 total coliform organisms per 100 millilitres of water, none of which should be fecal coliforms.

2. No consecutive samples from the same site should show the presence of coliform organisms.

3. For community drinking water supplies:

(a) not more than 10 per cent of the samples, based on a minimum of 10 samples, should show the presence of coliform organisms.

(b) not more than one sample from a set of samples taken from the community on a given day should show the presence of coliform organisms.

It is desirable that no virus or protozoa (such as Giardia) be detected.

Guidelines for radioactive substances in drinking water

Radionuclide	MAC (Bq/L)
Cesium-137	50
Iodine-131	10
Radium-226	1
Strontium-90	10
Tritium	40,000

MAC (Bq/L) refers to Maximum Acceptable Concentration in becquerels per litre. A becquerel (Bq) represents the radioactivity of material and the number of disintegrations per second.

Air pollution and health

Air pollutants, including acids, ozone, carbon monoxide and other chemicals, pose a threat to our health. Tiny droplets of acids, known as aerosols, are so light that they float in the air and so tiny that they can be drawn deep into the lungs. Tests have shown that children living in areas of high air pollution, such as southern Ontario, have more respiratory ailments and lower lung function than those living in cleaner regions such as the Prairies. Hospital admissions for respiratory ailments rise slightly during high pollution episodes in areas such as southern Ontario and Vancouver.

Expert advice

Advice on toxicology is available from a number of experts, including those in environment and health departments and in universities. In particular, there is the Canadian Network of Toxicology Centres, with centres in Guelph, Montreal and Saskatoon. One of the roles of this non-profit organization is to provide Canadians with information on toxicology. The main centre's telephone number, in Guelph, is (519) 837-3320. A full listing for the three centres can be found in the contacts section of this book.

SUSTAINABLE DEVELOPMENT

"Since 1900, the world's population has multiplied more than three times. Its economy has grown 20 fold. The consumption of fossil fuels has grown by a factor of 30, and industrial production by a factor of 50. Most of that growth, about four-fifths of it, occurred since 1950. Much of it is unsustainable. Earth's basic life-supporting capital of forests, species and soils is being depleted and its fresh waters and oceans are being degraded at an accelerating rate."— Beyond Interdependence: The Meshing of the World's Economy and the Earth's Ecology, by Jim MacNeill, Pieter Winsemius and Taizo Yakushiji.

The term "sustainable development" is the most controversial to hit the environmental world in recent history. It has created hope, inspiration, confusion and disagreement among many who try to grapple with the concept. Many government and business leaders have endorsed the concept, but the environmental movement is split. Some environmentalists say sustainable development is an idea that allows them to discuss environmental protection with industrialists, but others say the term is being used as a smokescreen by some companies that continue to pollute.

Some definitions of sustainable development

In its 1987 report, the World Commission on Environment and Development, the Brundtland Commission, called for "a new era of economic growth," but added that this era, "must be based on policies that sustain and expand the environmental resource base." The Brundtland Report defines sustainable development this way: "Humanity has the ability to make development sustainable — to ensure that it meets needs of the present without compromising the ability of future generations to meet their own needs." It went on to say that: "At a minimum, sustainable development must not endanger the natural systems that support life on earth: the waters, the soils and the living beings."

This definition is so broad that a number of people are claiming that they are practising sustainable development, while others say that the claims do not stand up. Some people have even twisted the term to "sustained economic development," which misses the environmental aspect. Members of the Brundtland Commission have made it clear that economic development will take place, particularly in poor nations, where hundreds of millions of people lack many of the necessities of a healthy life. Wherever it takes place, development must be controlled so that it does not destroy the environmental underpinnings of human civilization, and it must have more respect for the rights of other species of life to survive. Development must be sustainable on environmental, economic and social grounds.

The concept of sustainable development has been evolving through the 1980s, and Canada has been involved since the beginning. It was Canada, along with a handful of other nations, that pushed the United Nations to create the World Commission on Environment and Development, in 1984. In 1986, inspired by a visit from the commission, Canada's resource and environment ministers created a 17-member National Task Force on Environment and Economy. For the first time it brought environment ministers, industry leaders, environmentalists and academics to the same table. Their report said that Canada's, "long-term economic growth depends on a healthy environment." It said that, "environmental considerations cannot be an add-on, an afterthought. They must be made integral to economic policy making and planning, and a required element of any economic development proposal."

Based on recommendations of The National Task Force, the Prime Minister, provincial premiers and territorial leaders have all created high-level round tables on environment and economy to provide advice on how to move toward sustainable forms of development. A number of municipal round tables have been formed as well. Round table members typically include senior decision-makers from such sectors as government, industry, environment organizations, labour, academia and aboriginal peoples. Canada has also created the International Institute for Sustainable Development, in Winnipeg. The Federal and Quebec governments funded the creation of ECODECISION, an international journal on environment and development for decision-makers, based in Montreal.

Internationally, there are groups such as the Centre for Our Common Future, which was created to follow up the work of the Brundtland Commission, and the Business Council for Sustainable Development, both in Geneva. In June 1992, the Earth Summit, the United Nations Conference on Environment and Development, was held in Rio de Janeiro. The conference, headed by Canadian Maurice Strong, was the largest meeting of world leaders in history. The work of the conference will be carried on by the UN Commission on Sustainable Development. The major document to come out of the Earth Summit is Agenda 21, a blueprint for sustainable development at a global level. Its wide range of recommendations are aimed at governments, businesses and all levels of society. Journalists can get copies of the full document or a summary from the United Nations Department for Policy Coordination and Sustainable Development in New York. (See contact listings.)

In 1990, the federal government announced the nation's first ever Green Plan for a healthy environment, saying it was based upon the concept of sustainable development. The North American Free Trade Agreement among Canada, the United States and Mexico states that sustainable development is a legitimate objective for government policies. The terms sustainable and sustainability are cropping up in a number of stories, as people look for ways of doing business without excessive environmental damage. The challenge that sustainable development poses for government, business and individuals is in the implementation. First, people need to agree on a broad set of principles that will help to define what kinds and degrees of economic activity and personal consumption are sustainable. It will likely have to be a flexible formula, adjusted for increases in population and technological developments.

Clearly, a number of things we do today are not sustainable over the long term. Non-renewable resources, by definition, will not last forever, and once used up, there will be none for future generations. Some forms of pollution are unsustainable in an environmental sense. Destruction of the ozone layer is a clear case, and nations are acting to control this pollution. Virtually all economic development has some environmental impact. If one accepts the Brundtland definition that development should not compromise the ability of future generations to meet their needs, then many activities will have to be changed. It will not be an easy job.

• Ninety per cent of the world's commercial energy comes from non-renewable fossil fuels, mainly coal, oil and natural gas. Their production and burning adds greenhouse and acid gases to the atmosphere.

• Many farms now lose soil and organic matter faster than it is created, gradually undermining their ability to produce food. A number of farm irrigation systems are poisoning the soil through a process called salinization.

• Despite great increases in reforestation, Canada is still harvesting more wood than is replaced each year. The situation is much worse at a global level.

• In some areas, underground water supplies are being used up faster than nature can replace them.

• Fish are being caught faster than they can reproduce in a number of regions. This over-harvesting led to a shut-down of the northern cod fishery off Newfoundland in 1992.

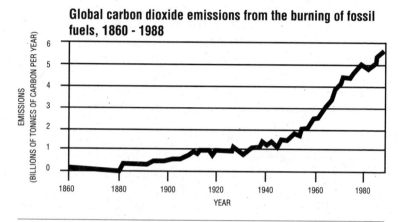

Global carbon dioxide emissions from the burning of fossil fuels, 1860 - 1988

Reproduced with permission from:
Government of Canada, *The State of Canada's Environment — 1991*, Ottawa, 1991.

It is important to draw the distinction between environmentally friendly and sustainable. A certain product may be called "friendly" because it is less damaging than a competitor. In order to determine if is more friendly and if it is sustainable over the long term, you need to analyze its entire life-cycle, including the extraction of raw materials to make the product, the amount and type of energy used in manufacture and transportation, the use of toxic materials in the life cycle, the effects of its use on the environment, and the impacts of disposal. Then you will get a clearer picture about whether it is degrading the environment. Naturally, many of our common products will show some environmentally unfriendly sides, but such life-cycle analysis will indicate which are the least damaging.

Some of the environmental damage can be reduced by relatively easy, though not always inexpensive, changes. We can make cars that are four times more fuel efficient than the average car sold today. We can build far more energy-efficient homes and factories. Some hazardous materials can be prevented from escaping into the environment, or can be replaced with safer alternatives. We can change economic policies and practices that stimulate short-term profits by using up resources or creating pollution. Based on the experience of cleaning up spills and old chemical dumps, most business and government leaders now accept the principle that it is wiser and cheaper to anticipate and prevent environmental problems than to react and try to cure the damage.

Groups such as the Brundtland Commission have said that the scope and scale of changes needed to achieve sustainability is so great that we must think of quite different forms of development and lifestyles. The changes can only be made if people deal with economics, culture, religion, politics, poverty and social justice. These are the factors that determine how many children people will have, how much of the earth's resources each person will want to consume, and how they value and treat the environment. This brings in a whole new set of commentators into the story. Ideas on sustainability are coming from economists, ethicists, political scientists, philosophers, social policy critics and foreign affairs analysts.

Carrying Capacity

There is no simple answer to the question: how many people can the earth support on a long-term basis? The carrying capacity of the environment is its ability to support life indefinitely, a concept that is not new. In 1883, William Forster Lloyd noted that a grazing area could feed animals as long as people did not try to graze too many cattle, thereby damaging the pasture and reducing the number of animals that it could sustain. Mr. Lloyd, a political economist, wrote that it was in the common interest of herdsmen to control the number of cattle, but not in their individual interest. As a result, each herdsman put more cattle on the pasture than it could support in order to maximize his personal gain. Mr. Lloyd called this the tragedy of the commons.

The planet faces a similar problem. We know that in our common interest we have to reduce some environmental impacts, such as damage to the ozone layer and over-fishing. The term carrying capacity is sometimes used in efforts to predict an ecologically sustainable human population.

The following are some estimates from various sources of the number people the planet could sustain:

- 6 billion with a vegetarian diet and food shared equally.
- 4 billion with 15 per cent of calories coming from animal products.
- 3 billion with 25 per cent of calories from animals.
- 2.5 billion with 35 per cent calories from animals, as in North America today.
- A relatively high standard of living might be enjoyed by all with a population of about 1 billion.

Only one of these estimates assumes that the current population of 5.4 billion is sustainable. None suggests that the planet can support more than 6 billion indefinitely, although that population figure will be surpassed by 1998.

Global equity

The Brundtland Report said that, at a global level, one of the greatest environmental problems is poverty. In order to pay even the interest on their foreign debts, some poor nations use up their limited natural resources, cutting down forests, over-farming and over-grazing the land. More than one quarter of Central America's rain forests have been cut or burned since 1960 for cattle ranching, and 85 to 95 per cent of the beef goes to North America for hamburger, tinned meat and pet food. Meanwhile, the consumption of beef per person has fallen in Central America. The forces behind world poverty are many and complex. Some lie in the hands of those who have economic, military and political power in poor nations, and who spend billions of dollars on palaces, limousines and high-tech weapons. But other economic forces are beyond the control of the poor. For example, the prices of many commodities produced by poor nations, ranging from cotton to oil, have fallen in recent years.

According to the United Nations Development Programme, the richest one fifth of the world gets 83 per cent of the world's income, while the poorest fifth gets 1.4 per cent. Despite foreign aid programs, the poor are getting poorer and poor nations are sending more money to the rich, mainly in debt repayments, than they are receiving in assistance. There are growing calls from poor nations to have a greater share of the benefits of industrialization, and the right to pollute to some degree. If such rights and benefits were to be distributed more equally and, at the same time, some environmental impacts were to be reduced, this would require a major shift in consumption and pollution patterns. A closing statement from the June 1992 Earth Summit in Rio de Janeiro called for: "the transition

Distribution of economic activity, 1989 — percentage of world total (Quintiles of population ranked by income)

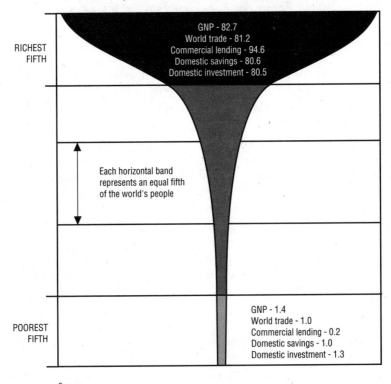

RICHEST FIFTH

GNP - 82.7
World trade - 81.2
Commercial lending - 94.6
Domestic savings - 80.6
Domestic investment - 80.5

Each horizontal band represents an equal fifth of the world's people

POOREST FIFTH

GNP - 1.4
World trade - 1.0
Commercial lending - 0.2
Domestic savings - 1.0
Domestic investment - 1.3

Source:
UNDP, _Human Development Report -- 1992_, New York, 1992

to patterns of production and consumption in industrialized countries which would significantly reduce their disproportionate contribution to deterioration of the earth's environment."

The Prime Minister of Malaysia put the case bluntly when he told the world that his country had the right to exploit its forests, just as Europe and North America had cut and are still cutting much of their virgin timber to build their economies. The problem faced by the world is that if every country exploits its resources and produces pollution to the maximum extent possible for economic growth, the shared global environment will suffer. This would be the tragedy of the global commons.

Some principles of sustainability

The shift to a more environmentally sustainable society, with its changes in lifestyles and economic activity, needs to operate on some different values, using different principles.

The National Round Table on the Environment and the Economy has produced the following Objectives for Sustainable Development, with a preamble:

The natural world and its component life forms and the ability of that world to regenerate itself through its own evolution has basic value. Within and among human societies, fairness, equality, diversity and self-reliance are pervasive characteristics of development that is sustainable.

1. STEWARDSHIP
We must preserve the capacity of the biosphere to evolve by managing our social and economic activities for the benefit of present and future generations.

2. SHARED RESPONSIBILITY
Everyone shares the responsibility for a sustainable society. All sectors must work toward this common purpose, with each being accountable for its decisions and actions, in a spirit of partnership and open co-operation.

3. PREVENTION AND RESILIENCE

We must try to anticipate and prevent future problems by avoiding the negative environmental, economic, social and cultural impacts of policies, programs, decisions and development activities. Recognizing that there will always be environmental and other events which we cannot anticipate, we should also strive to increase social, economic and environmental resilience in the face of change.

4. CONSERVATION

We must maintain and enhance essential ecological processes, biological diversity and life support systems of our environment and natural resources.

5. ENERGY AND RESOURCE MANAGEMENT

Overall, we must reduce the energy and resource content of growth, harvest renewable resources on a sustainable basis, and make wise and efficient use of our non-renewable resources.

6. WASTE MANAGEMENT

We must first endeavour to reduce the production of waste, then re-use, recycle and recover waste by-products of our industrial and domestic activities.

7. REHABILITATION AND RECLAMATION

Our future policies, programs and development must endeavour to rehabilitate and reclaim damaged environments.

8. SCIENTIFIC AND TECHNOLOGICAL INNOVATION

We must support education, and research and development of technologies, goods and services essential to maintaining environmental quality, social and cultural values and economic growth.

9. INTERNATIONAL RESPONSIBILITY

We must think globally when we act locally. Global responsibility requires ecological interdependence among provinces and nations, and an obligation to accelerate the integration of environmental, social, cultural and economic goals. By working co-operatively within Canada and internationally, we can develop comprehensive and equitable solutions to problems.

77

10. GLOBAL DEVELOPMENT

Canada should support methods that are consistent with the preceding objectives when assisting developing nations.

The Ontario Round Table on Environment and Economy produced six principles of sustainable development:

1. ANTICIPATION AND PREVENTION

Anticipating and preventing problems is better than trying to react and fix them after they occur.

2. FULL-COST ACCOUNTING

Accounting must reflect all long-term environmental and economic costs, not just those of the current market.

3. INFORMED DECISION-MAKING

The best decisions are those based on sound, accurate and up-to-date information.

4. LIVING OFF THE INTEREST

We must live off the interest our environment provides, and not destroy its capital base.

5. QUALITY OVER QUANTITY

The quality of social and economic development must take precedence over quantity.

6. RESPECT FOR NATURE AND THE RIGHTS OF FUTURE GENERATIONS

We must respect nature and the rights of future generations.

The following are further goals, drawn from a number of sources:

• Protect the basic needs of clean air, fresh water, healthy food, shelter and sanitation and medical care.

• Create less pollution per capita and in total.

• More local and regional self-reliance (bioregionalism), especially for goods which require a lot of energy to move. For example, use more solar (local) energy, dispose of wastes locally, grow more food locally, and live within the local water supply.

• Use renewable resources within their ability to renew themselves and without depleting underlying resources, such as soil fertility or the ability of forests to re-grow and fish to maintain stable populations.

• Use non-renewable resources in most economical manner that is feasible.

• Maintain ecological processes and life support systems essential to human health and well being. These include ecological succession, soil regeneration and protection, the recycling of nutrients and the cleansing of air and water.

• Preserve genetic diversity, which forms the basis of life on earth, and assures our foods, many medicines and industrial products. It means respecting the interests of other species in the long-term interest of humanity.

It is perhaps fitting to give the last thoughts on sustainability to someone from a country facing enormous development challenges. The following is excerpted from a guest editorial by Rajesh Tandon in the September-October 1992 issue of *Development Alternatives*, published in New Delhi:

"Sustainable development is essentially a matter of achieving a sustainable lifestyle, based on meeting the basic needs of all people, on austerity and economy, and deriving satisfaction from existing socio-spiritual processes in society. Viewed in this sense, the contemporary lifestyle of the bulk of the population in the countries of the North, as well as the blind aping by the upwardly mobile classes in the countries of the South, is blatantly unsustainable. A lifestyle based on pursuit of material goods for the sake of over-consumption, and of living only in the present without reference to the past or concern for the future, is at the root of current unsustainable lifestyles. Sustainable development can only be built on the basis of a sustainable lifestyle."

SECTION TWO
ENVIRONMENTAL JOURNALISM

Environmental journalism in Canada has evolved slowly and erratically over a long period of time. The roots of what we now call environment reporting were laid down during the nineteenth century with stories about parks and wildlife. Until the last few decades, most writing about the natural environment was "nature writing," either from the viewpoint of hunters and fishers, or from that of people who wanted to preserve species and wild lands for purely aesthetic reasons. Such stories appeared mainly on the outdoors pages or in nature and bird-watching columns.

Modern environmental journalism started in the early 1960s, when Rachel Carson's book *Silent Spring* raised the issue of risks from such chemicals as DDT. In 1970, Canadian journalists had the first big story about threats to human health from toxic materials in the environment, when mercury was found in fish from a number of regions, mainly in Ontario. During the late 1970s, stories about other hazardous materials, such as PCBs, made the news. The next big story was acid rain, which gathered steam during the mid-1970s. During the 1980s, the environmental agenda exploded. Journalists suddenly had to deal with a host of complex issues, such as logging, pulp and paper, the ozone layer, population growth, the loss of species and climate change. Each region of the country had its story. Almost everyone had a worrisome dump in their region. Many regions faced conflicts over logging, pulp mills and hydro dams. Nuclear energy periodically became a story, particularly after the Chernobyl accident in the Soviet Union in 1986. With the Brundtland Report of 1987, journalists suddenly had to learn the lingo of economics, and try to relate economic decision-making to environmental impacts.

There were a few environment reporters in the 1960s, but media interest in the subject waxed and waned as crises flared up then died from the news. Now, all media outlets must cover the environment, even if they simply try to keep up with local problems, such as where the next landfill is going. A growing number of papers, radio and television stations have designated an environment specialist. In these outlets, the environment beat is often a split beat, with the journalist also responsible for another one or two issues, such as science, medicine, agriculture, forestry or natural resources.

Environmental journalism still suffers the weakness of being considered a junior posting by many editors. If journalists do well in this field, they are often "promoted" to something considered more prestigious, such as political reporting. As a result, environment reporting often suffers from the revolving door syndrome. This means the environment reporter is frequently still learning the complex issues when he or she is posted elsewhere. Even if reporters understand the issues, editors often lack the knowledge to catch factual errors, or give environmental stories the appropriate play. Some professional organizations are trying to help journalists understand environment issues. They include the Canadian Association of Journalists, Canadian Science Writers' Association, and the U.S.-based Society of Environmental Journalists and Scientists' Institute for Public Information. (See Media Organizations in the Contacts section.) The University of Western Ontario has created a short summer course, Environmental Issues for Journalists.

One of the most difficult aspects of environmental journalism is that it involves science reporting, and most journalists have no training in this field. As a result, the media often fail to understand the limits of science, and reporters too often demand immediate and definitive answers, when none is possible. Journalists have to understand that the role of science is as much to pose questions as to answer them. In many cases, particularly in newly emerging issues, there are no quick and easy answers about whether a given substance or activity is hazardous. Research into toxicity can take years. However such long scientific research projects clash with the reporter's demand for news on the hour. This means that many stories have to be written without a final answer. The challenge is to communicate to the public what level of certainty surrounds each statement, and to try to explain the qualifications of the sources quoted. When the jury is out on a story, it is important to draw on different viewpoints.

The acid rain story is a good example. In the mid-1970s, a few researchers said that some lakes were becoming acidic, and that this was killing fish. They said the acid fallout came from industrial smokestacks, often tens or even hundreds of kilometres away from the lakes, and also from the tailpipes of all motor vehicles. The researchers had presented deformed fish and acidic water from the lakes as evidence. They had a theory that the acidity came from gases that blew in from a number of sources. Governments and industries were reluctant to accept the idea that industrial and automobile pollution was killing lakes, and that it would cost hundreds of millions of dollars to reduce the emissions. Journalists were getting a lot of conflicting signals from different "reliable" sources. During the latter 1970s and into the early 1980s, the scientific evidence kept mounting until governments and industries agreed that acid rain was a real problem and that it had to be controlled. The story shifted to one of how tough governments would be in setting clean-up deadlines, and who would pay the tab. By the mid-1980s, there was a national consensus in Canada on the amount of pollution to be reduced, the deadlines, and who would pay.

This same slow process has been played out in a number of cases, such as CFCs damaging the ozone layer, DDT causing the death of birds, and greenhouse gases posing a risk of climate warming. In each case, journalists had to explain the science as it emerged, and try to draw rational conclusions. In cases such as acid rain and the ozone layer, the media coverage has generally reflected the scientific consensus as it emerged. Every so often the media go off the mark, and fail to present a consistent and coherent picture. One example of journalists misreading the science involves many of the stories on PCBs. Once released into the environment, PCBs build up in the food chain and cause harm to wildlife. There is evidence that even relatively low levels of PCBs may cause some harm to humans, if taken in through the food chain. Some stories about PCBs have left the impression they are so highly toxic that just having them in the neighbourhood poses a threat to life. This kind of story is not based on sound science, has caused needless public fears and discredits good environment reporting.

SOURCES

One of the most difficult problems for journalists is knowing whom to rely on for advice in controversial stories. Governments are often the first stop for the journalist seeking environmental information. Departments of environment, agriculture, fisheries, forestry, mining, energy, transport and health set the rules for environmental performance on everything from discharges by big factories and emissions from cars to levels of timber and fish harvests, and use of pesticides. Governments investigate and enforce the laws, and are responsible for conducting environmental assessments. Governments publish reams of reports and most of this material is public, but so much environmental information has been written over the years that one of the greatest challenges for a journalist is to simply locate the right documents for the story. While governments are supposed to be the independent arbiters on environmental issues, they often get drawn into taking different sides. Sometimes economic development or job creation policies override environmental considerations.

Most environment groups were formed to pressure companies and governments to reduce pollution and protect natural resources. These organizations are collectively known as non-government organizations (NGOs.) Most of them are highly accessible to the news media because this is their most effective way of communicating a message, bringing pressure on governments or industries and raising public support for their causes. Most of the 2,000 or so environment groups in Canada are small, and focus mainly on lobbying on a specific local issue. However, some groups have become large and quite sophisticated. They publish detailed reports on complex issues, ranging from chemicals to wildlife, and the work of the best ones is so good that it is even quoted by governments. NGOs frequently make the news when they raise an issue or when they respond as critics to statements by government and business. For many years, NGOs could only have an impact on environmental policies by criticizing from the outside, and some groups retain that position. Other NGOs are spending more time at the negotiating table with business and government, working out agreements on how to make the economy more environmentally sustainable. While these environmentalists are pleased to have a seat at the negotiating table, they sometimes worry that they are not achieving as much as they would like in return for their participation. They also fear a loss of public support if they are no longer seen as attacking the polluters, through the news media.

It used to be that what was good for business was considered good for society. This attitude changed starting in the 1960s, when sectors of industry were linked to a number of unpopular issues including the Vietnam war, faulty consumer products and toxic pollution. Most business people reacted to public criticism of their environmental performance by saying they knew best how to deal with issues like pollution and the use of natural resources. Over the past decade, a growing number business leaders realized this position was unacceptable to the public, and they had to improve their environmental performance. The concept of sustainable development gave business people a term that let them feel more comfortable talking about the environment, because the term was linked with the economy, where they felt more at home. In recent years, some progressive ideas about changing the face of development to make it more environmentally sustainable have been coming from the business community. A number of businesses and business organizations are now acting as information sources for the media, and publishing candid reports of their environmental performance. The incentive for change is even stronger on business than on government. Companies can be regulated, fined, sued or boycotted to a punishing degree.

Academics have experience in fields ranging from acid rain to zoology, as well as economics, political science, environmental ethics and sustainable development. They are often the original source of research that turns up such problems as acid rain and damage to the ozone layer. It is worth noting that not all academics are totally independent from those who create or deal with environmental problems. Some teachers receive grants, or work under contract for government or business. In such cases, this does not mean their opinions are not useful, simply that they are involved with one of the actors in the field. University and college information officers can usually provide names of experts in a wide range of fields. There are a number of other sources of information and commentary on environmental issues, including first nations, churches, unions and economists.

ENVIRONMENT REPORTING AND THE ECOSYSTEM CONCEPT

Few journalists have any formal training in environmental sciences, and it takes time to learn enough of the basics so that you can follow complex issues. One of the most useful concepts to grasp is the ecosystem concept. What is an ecosystem? It can be defined as a given area in which living organisms have a stable relationship. One can refer to the ecosystem of a lake, river, forest, a large region, or the entire planet. The planetary ecosystem is sometimes called the ecosphere or biosphere.

The ecosystem concept is a reference to the close interrelationships between components of an ecosystem. If you remove too much of one component, this can cause short or long-term damage to other parts. The ecosystem concept is also used to explain linkages. It is because air, water, land and life have such a close relationship, that chemicals that were supposed to "stay put" in one area turn up in food and drinking water somewhere else. If you understand ecosystem concept, you will understand why there is no safe place to dump toxic wastes, and why cutting down too many trees, draining too many wetlands or changing the atmosphere will have negative effects in ways that are often difficult to predict.

SITE VISITS

There is an understandable tendency to do a lot of environmental reporting by reading scientific documents and following up with telephone interviews. It is important for journalists to get into the field to see the issues first-hand. Most people have no idea what a water or sewage treatment plant looks like from the inside. Few journalists have seen a toxic waste treatment plant, or walked through a forestry operation to see both the impact of clear-cutting and the techniques used to regenerate forests. The first time you walk through a pulp and paper mill or a chemical complex and look at the giant machines, you will get an

The movement of key elements (e.g., carbon, nitrogen, sulphur, and phosphorus) through the Ecosphere

The atmosphere, the most mobile component of the Ecosphere, facilitates exchanges between living and non-living things, between life forms, and between generations

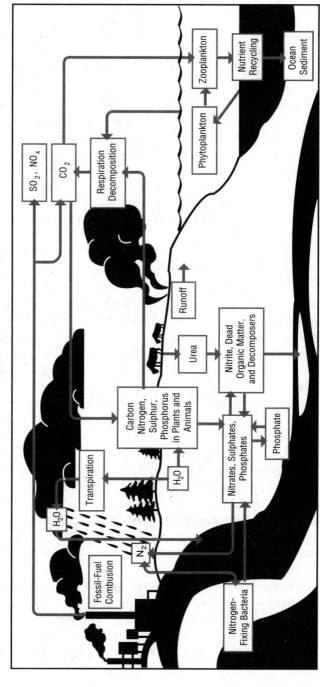

Reproduced with permission from: Government of Canada, *The State of Canada's Environment — 1991*, Ottawa, 1991.

entirely different appreciation for the job of changing equipment to control pollution. Government laboratories are the source of information about the levels of toxic chemicals. Visits to landfills and recycling plants will show where waste goes, and what happens to it. It is also vital to see nature in a natural state, to walk in a forest, prairie or wetland to see why they are important to our environmental health. There are lots of tours available from people eager to show one side or the other of a given story, and they can provide valuable advice and opinions about what needs to be done.

ANALYZING ENVIRONMENTAL CHOICES FOR GREEN CONTENT

Journalists are faced with claims that some products are environmentally friendly. In many cases, the products represent an advance, but products may be less green than they seem. The backers of a product may say it is environmentally friendly because it does not contain one hazardous substance, but fail to mention it has other harmful impacts. As people try to define what activities are more sustainable, they begin to realize how difficult a task that really is. Journalists need to understand the concept of life cycle analysis, including the direct impact of the product and its side effects. Take beverage containers as an example.

• Bottles are made of sand that must be extracted and made into glass using energy. Bottles are heavy, and require fuel to move them to and from the consumer. If thrown away, they add to the litter problem or help to fill dumps. If re-used this avoids cost of breaking them down to be re-melted, but they must be washed, and this requires energy and soap and produces sewage waste.

• Aluminium cans are made from bauxite that must be mined, creating wastes, and transported, using energy. Smelting aluminium requires large amounts of electrical energy and produces wastes. Aluminium cans are not re-used, but can be recycled. This requires some energy, though much less than smelting bauxite. If thrown away, cans become litter, and if put in landfills, they take up space, though less than glass bottles.

• Paper and multiple layer packs involving paper, plastic and aluminium foil require the manufacture of a number of materials. The production of paper requires cutting trees, and pulp and paper mills discharge chemical waste into waterways. The other materials also have environmental impacts. The containers cannot be re-used, but, where plants exist, they are being crushed and bonded to form a wood replacement. In landfills, they take up less space than bottles or cans.

Wading through the layers of questions is not easy. A number of environmental and industry groups provide advice on the environmental impacts of various products. The Environmental Choice Program, created by Environment Canada, is to help consumers identify goods and services that reduce the burden on the environment. The program is managed by an multi-sectoral board, and technical advice is provided by the Canadian Standards Association. The program sells producers the right to display the EcoLogo, an image of three doves intertwined to form a maple leaf, on products that have been approved. By late 1992 the program has published criteria for 41 product types, covering more than 700 products from 130 companies. These include insulation made from recycled paper, reduced-pollution paints, recycled writing paper, water-saving plumbing fixtures and re-refined motor oil.

CLANGERS — WATCH OUT FOR THESE

We all fall into the trap of using imprecise terms that seem to tell the story. Sometimes the myth becomes part of popular folklore. In environmental terms, some examples are:

THE FAMOUS STYROFOAM CUP THAT NEVER WAS

Styrofoam is a trademark of the Dow Chemical Co. It is an extruded polystyrene plastic foam that is produced in large blue slabs as an insulating material used mainly in construction. You sometimes see blue Styrofoam slabs on the walls of partially-finished buildings. Despite popular wisdom, and thousands of stories, Styrofoam was never used for foam plastic cups, plates or food containers. Polystyrene foam plastic is the generic name for the white foam plastic used in coffee cups and food containers. In Canada, these containers are no longer made using CFCs.

CFCS IN AEROSOL SPRAY CANS

This is a popular image for stories on the destruction of the ozone layer, particularly on television. CFCs are still used in sprays in some nations, but Canada, the United States and a number of nations have banned CFCs in virtually all aerosols. The only exception in Canada is for some medical sprays, and this is likely to be phased out.

GOOD AND BAD OZONE: WHICH OZONE LAYER WAS THAT?

To use the language of some scientists, there is good ozone and bad ozone. Stratospheric (good) ozone is what protects us from excess UV-B radiation. Ground-level (bad) ozone is formed by air pollutants from cars, industries and other sources, and it harms our lungs and plant life. Both ozone stories involve the same molecule, O^3, but the two ozone layers are physically far apart. Unfortunately, ground-level ozone does not drift up into the sky to repair the hole in the stratospheric ozone layer.

OZONE DEPLETION AND GREENHOUSE EFFECT

A number of journalists confuse these two atmospheric issues in stories. One reason is that CFCs destroy the ozone layer, and they are also a greenhouse gas that can cause climate warming. To make things even more confusing, scientists believe that ozone depletion in the lower stratosphere may be cooling the planet, partially offsetting global warming. As CFCs are controlled to protect the ozone layer, climate warming may accelerate. Another gas, nitrous oxide, is a pollutant from combustion, and it both destroys the ozone layer and acts as a greenhouse gas.

WHOSE BRAND IS THAT?

One chemical company official reports with some chagrin that she fielded a call from a teacher wanting to know what people should do if a truck of dioxin overturned. In fact, dioxins are trace contaminants, that are rarely found in quantities greater than a few parts per billion. Dioxin had been in the news so much that the teacher though it was a brand-name product.

QUESTIONS TO ASK

There is no magic test for environmental sustainability, but there are some tests that can be applied. If you ask the following questions (and others that you can develop) you will get a sense of whether a new product, project or idea is more or less environmentally damaging than the alternatives.

- Is it sustainable in that it can be carried on indefinitely without running down its resource base? Can that claim be proven?

- Will this project or program use up non-renewable resources, such as fossil fuels? (Will it use them at a greater or lesser rate than some alternative program?)

- Will it use renewable resources at a rate greater than natural replacement? (What is the quality of replacement? For example, will the wood of new trees be as good as the old, and will it be ready in time for need?)

- Does it erode or degrade soil?

- Does it reduce available fresh water supplies?

- Does it reduce food supplies?

- Does it pollute the air, land or water?

- Does it damage the ozone layer?

- Does it add greenhouse gases to the atmosphere?

- Does it result in more or less garbage?

- Does it reduce the diversity of living species?
- Does it release toxic substances into the environment?
  - Are they persistent toxic substances?
  - Do they bioaccumulate and build up in the food chain?
  - What are their breakdown products in the environment or our bodies?
  - What is known about their health effects in humans, wildlife or test animals?
    - short-term effects: death, injury, sickness.
    - long term effects: cancer, mutations, birth defects, reproductive effects, genetic changes, neurological effects, immune system suppression, damage to organs, etc.
  - What standards or guidelines exist in any jurisdiction (domestic or foreign) for allowable concentrations in our bodies, food, air, water, etc.

In many cases, there will be no easy answers for these questions. No product will come through such a screen showing zero impact. The challenge is to find those which are least environmentally damaging, and to find a mix of products which, in total, will not put too heavy a strain on the biosphere. A number of groups, including some within Environment Canada, the National Round Table and some universities, are developing environmental indicators as a way of tracking progress on the environment. You can maintain your own set of indicators on any given issue, simply by collecting data that is available from official sources. At a national level, there are records on the emissions of a number of harmful pollutants, the rate of reforestation and the state of fishery stocks, to mention a few. At a local level, you can obtain figures on the amount of garbage produced in total and per person in your municipality. You can track the use of energy and water. These are all indicators of environmental impacts.

Environmental reporting and objectivity

According to Emil Salim, Indonesia's environment minister and a member of the Brundtland Commission, "...the mass media plays an important and strategic role in promoting public awareness and shaping its attitude in favour of sustainable development."

Many people say the media should provide leadership on environmental issues, and push people to change their behaviour, just as the media do on other issues, such as crime and drug abuse. This puts the media on the spot. Everyone can agree that crime and drugs are serious problems, but a lot of the environmental damage is the result of activities, such as using cars, that we consider a normal part of life. And which side should the reporter take on clear-cutting — that of the logger who wants a job or the environmentalist who is talking about leaving a natural legacy for the future? Reporters sometimes find themselves being pushed to take sides. One way of approaching these issues is to take the position of a disinterested observer — not there to side with one group or another. However, you are not uninterested. The health of the environment, including humans, and the resources on which we base our economy, is at stake, and journalists have a duty to fairly and accurately explain risks and alternatives to people.

The next stages

Over the past three decades, environment reporting has broadened and deepened, but it is still seen by many as a niche specialty. We will always need journalists who have the time to dig into the environmental sciences and explain the nuts and bolts of complex issues, such as the greenhouse effect. This kind of reporting, which is often categorized as the bad news beat, provides only half the story. There is great need for stories that provide answers to the questions that are always being raised by environmental science. The next step for environmental journalism needs to be a long one. It means dealing with economic policies and political choices, with cultural values and the beliefs of a society. It will require not just environment reporters who can write about these subjects, but political, economic and other specialists who understand environmental impacts and can work these into their normal reporting.

SECTION THREE
REFERENCE

ENVIRONMENTAL TERMS AND GRAMMAR

Concentrations

It is important to understand that pollution discharges are allowed based on what regulators consider to be acceptable concentrations in the environment. In some cases, you will be given information saying that a source is allowed to discharge so many parts per million of a contaminant in the air and water. One part per million may seem unimportant. However, if a source is discharging one million tonnes of waste water per year, it means that one tonne of the pollutant can legally be released, so it is important to ask how much is being released. If the contaminant is a persistent toxic substance, the amount in the environment will gradually increase, and if the substance bioaccumulates, then it can build up in the food chain. Be careful not to mix up discharges of waste water with discharges of waste. It is not the amount of water discharged that is polluting the environment, it is the amount of waste in the water.

Zero discharge and virtual elimination

The terms zero discharge and virtual elimination are often ill-defined. Under the 1978 Great Lakes Water Quality Agreement, Canada and the United States said that it was their policy that:

"The discharge of toxic substances in toxic amounts be prohibited and the discharge of any or all persistent toxic substances be virtually eliminated."

The agreement said that, "regulatory strategies for controlling or preventing the input of persistent toxic substances to the Great Lakes System shall be adopted in accordance with the following principles:

Simplified Great Lakes food web

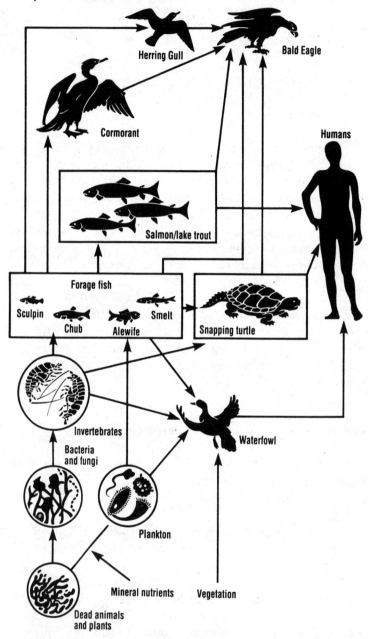

"The intent of programs specified in this annex is to virtually eliminate the input of persistent toxic substances...

"The philosophy adopted for control of inputs of persistent toxic substances shall be zero discharge."

The definition of "persistent" used in the Great Lakes context is that the hazardous substance does not break down to at least half the original amount within eight weeks. There have been many discussions about exactly what the above phrases mean. A number of people interpret them to mean that there should be no use of persistent toxic substances, because experience has shown some will almost always leak or be spilled into the environment. The term "zero" is used in a number of regulations, but as ever more accurate detection equipment is invented, zero detectable moves down from parts per million to parts per billion, trillion, quadrillion and quintillion. At that point, many scientists question whether the level of pollution would be high enough to have any adverse effects. Some people say that the term zero can be interpreted to mean that substances can be discharged if they have zero effect on living organisms. There is another aspect to the interpretation of zero discharge. Because so much pollution is now present in the water, some of it will be taken in by industries that are downstream from sources of pollution. Some people say the term zero discharge should be interpreted to mean zero pollution added to the discharge, as it goes through a process, such as an industrial plant.

Some contentious phrases

• *Scientifically Unproved* — This term is used by some people who want to delay taking action on a potential environmental problem. The role of science is to ask questions. As a result there will likely always be some scientists who are questioning assumptions. This does not mean that decisions on relative risk cannot be made until there is scientific unanimity. If this were the case, few decisions would ever be made. So be careful in weighing scientific advice not casually to let one scientist's opinion easily override that of a number of scientists. Also, check to see what qualifications a scientist in one field has to comment on issues in fields where he or she may have little experience.

• *Not Found* — In scientific reports, you will sometimes see the letters ND, meaning that the substance was not detected. As indicated in the section on zero discharge (above), the ability to detect depends on the sensitivity of the equipment being used. By failing to use the right equipment or techniques, people can avoid finding pollutants. In one case during the 1980s, water samples were being taken in a lake that was known to be contaminated with hundreds of chemicals, but researchers said that they were only finding one pollutant — iron. Upon questioning, the researchers said that they were not given enough money to use equipment sensitive enough to detect the other chemicals.

MEASUREMENTS AND TINY NUMBERS

Metric to Imperial Measure (approximate figures)

LENGTH

1 centimetre = 0.39 inches
1 metre = 3.28 feet
1 kilometre = 0.62 miles

AREA

1 square yard = 0.836 square metres
1 square metre = 1.196 square yards
1 hectare (10,000 square metres) = 2.47 acres
1 acre = 0.404 hectares
1 square kilometre (100 hectares) = 0.38 square miles
1 square mile = 2.59 square kilometres
1 square kilometre = 247 acres = 0.386 square miles

WEIGHT

1 ounce = 28.35 grams	1 gram = 0.035 ounces
1 pound = 453.59 grams	1 kilogram = 2.2 pounds
1 ton = 0.907 tonnes	1 tonne = 1.102 tons

LIQUID WEIGHT

1 Imperial gallon of water = 10 pounds = 4.536 kilograms
1 U.S. gallon of water = 8.33 pounds = 3.78 kilograms

(The weight of water can be used for converting volumes of most liquid wastes that are highly diluted in water, such as municipal sewage and most industrial effluents.)

Sewage sludge and industrial sludge:
1 Imperial gallon (4.5 litres) is closer to 12-13 pounds or 5-6 kilograms

Mineral oil, as in PCBs:
1 Imperial gallon (4.5 litres) is closer to 8 pounds (3.6 kilograms)

VOLUME — Dry

1 cubic inch = 16.387 cubic centimetres
1 cubic centimetre = 0.061 cubic inches
1 cubic foot = 23,317 cubic centimetres or .028 cubic metre
1 cubic metre = 35.7 cubic feet = 1.308 cubic yards
1 cubic yard = 0.764 cubic metres

VOLUME — Liquid

1 litre = 0.22 Imperial gallons (0.26 U.S. gallons)
1 Imperial gallon = 1.2 U.S. gal = 4.546 litres
1 U.S. gallon = .832 Imperial gal = 3.78 litres
1 cubic metre = 1,000 litres
1 cubic kilometre = 0.24 cubic miles
1 cubic kilometre = 1 billion cubic metres = 1 trillion litres
1 cubic mile = 4.1 cubic kilometres

Water volumes for irrigation and export:
1 acre foot =1,233.5 cubic metres

SYMBOLS FOR BIG AND SMALL NUMBERS

exa E	1 quintillion 10^{18}
peta P	1 quadrillion 10^{15}
tera T	1 trillion 10^{12}
giga G	1 billion 10^{9}
mega M	1 million 10^{6}
kilo k	1,000 10^{3}
hecto h	100 10^{2}
deca da	10
deci d	1 tenth 10^{-1}
centi c	1 hundredth 10^{-2}
milli m	1 thousandth 10^{-3}
micro μ	1 millionth 10^{-6}
nano n	1 billionth 10^{-9}
pico p	1 trillionth 10^{-12}
femto f	1 quadrillionth 10^{-15}
atto a	1 quintillionth 10^{-18}

TINY PARTS

• ***ppm*** means parts per million. For example, 1 ppm of a pollutant means there is one gram of a pollutant in a million grams (1 tonne) of the material tested, or one litre of pollutant in a million litres of water.

• ***ppb*** means parts per billion
• ***ppt*** means parts per trillion
• ***ppq*** means parts per quadrillion

(Each one of these is 1,000 times smaller than the preceding factor.)

• ***ppmv*** - parts per million by volume
• ***ppmdv*** - parts per million by dry volume
• ***dl*** - decilitre
• μ***eq/l*** - micro equivalent per litre

100

- 1 milligram (mg)   1/1,000 of a gram
- 1 millimetre   1/1,000 of a metre
- 1 micrometre μm   1 millionth of a metre
- (1/10,000 of a mm)
- milligrams per kilogram   ppm
- milligrams per litre   ppm
- micrograms per litre (μg/l)   ppb
- micrograms per gram (μg/g)   ppb
- nanograms per litre   ppt
- nanograms per gram   ppt
- micrograms per kilogram (μg/kg)   ppt
- picograms per litre   ppq
- picograms per gram   ppq

SOME COMPARISONS TO SHOW THE RELATIVE SIZE OR AMOUNT OF A POLLUTANT IN THE ENVIRONMENT

1 part per thousand of table salt makes water somewhat unpalatable.

1 ppm
- 1 second in 277 hours or 11.5 days
- 1 minute in two years
- swimmers can detect chlorine in a pool at 1 ppm

1 ppb
- 1 second in 32 years
- enough for a human nose to detect the smell of a rose
- fuel oil can be detected by a sensitive nose
- 80 ppb of ozone in the air over eight hours can cause health problems
- humans need a minimum of 1 ppb per day Vitamin B12 to survive

1 ppt
- 1 second in 32,000 years (320 centuries)
- 1 grain of salt in an Olympic size swimming pool
- 1 small gnat's wing in a 100 tonne whale
- the width of one hair in a belt around the world
- 20 ppt is limit for 2,3,7,8-TCDD dioxin in fish for human consumption

1 ppq	• 1 second in 32,000,000 years.
	• 1/1,000 of that small gnat's wing in a 100 tonne whale
	• dioxin can be detected at 5 ppq by sensitive equipment

WATER CONSUMPTION AND USE

The per capita use of water in Canada is a bit more than 4,100 litres of water per day, while the U.S. demand runs at 6,300 litres a head. This includes total water use in each nation, most of it for power generation, industrial cooling and processing, and agricultural irrigation.

The average Canadian personally uses an average of 285 litres per day at home, for drinking, cooking, washing and sanitation. That national average varies from 90 to 320 litres a person, depending upon whether it is drawn from a limited supply in a rural well or from a powerful city supply, and whether or not there is a large lawn to water.

An adult's minimum daily biological need for water is an average of 1.34 litres in drink, and another two-thirds of a litre in food. The rest is used and disposed of by our machines:

• A flush toilet uses 20 litres
• A shower uses about 25 litres a minute
• A bathtub holds about 130 litres
• A dishwasher uses about 65 litres
• A clothes washer uses about 230 litres
• A garden hose uses 1,500 litres or more an hour
• A dripping tap wastes from 30 to 100 litres a day and, on average, water leaks account for 5 to 10 per cent of the water use in North American homes.

FORESTRY STATISTICS

Planting rates for seedlings
•Re-planting varies from 1,800 to 2,500 trees per hectare, and produces about 600 to 700 mature trees per hectare, after some trees die and others are thinned out.

Impacts of paper recycling
•It takes about 19 mature softwood trees, such as spruce, to produce 1 tonne of pulp or paper. This is enough about 2,000 daily newspapers, each weighing 500 grams.

•It takes 43 per cent less energy to recycle paper, than to process raw wood.

•The manufacture of recycled paper requires 29,200 litres less water per tonne than new paper.

•Recycling paper reduces air pollution emissions by 30 kilograms per tonne. Every tree standing absorbs an average of 4 kilograms of carbon dioxide per year.

•Recycling one tonne of paper instead of dumping it saves 2.5 cubic metres of landfill space.

•In 1991, Canada used about 6 million tonnes of paper. About 25 per cent was recycled.

CANS AND BOTTLES —
ALUMINIUM, STEEL AND GLASS

•Making aluminium from recycled scrap cuts energy use and air pollution by 95 per cent.

•It takes 10 per cent of the energy to make copper from scrap rather than from ore.

•It takes about half the energy to make steel from scrap rather than from raw ore. Every tonne of steel recycled saves more than 1.5 tonnes of iron ore.

•The energy saved by recycling one glass bottle will light a 100-watt bulb for 4 hours.

RADIATION

Radiation exists in many forms, some very dangerous and some apparently not dangerous. At the dangerous or high energy end of the spectrum, are alpha, beta, gamma, and x-ray radiation. These are called ionizing radiation, because they can electrically charge (ionize) material. Their high energy can damage cells, initiate cancers and even kill in a very short time. When ionizing radiation hits other materials, it knocks electrons loose from molecules, forming electrically charged atoms or groups of atoms called ions. These ions can have harmful effects, such as altering DNA molecules, and causing tumors.

Non-ionizing radiation has less energy than ionizing radiation. It lacks enough energy to dislodge electrons, but some forms of non-ionizing radiation, such as microwaves, are strong enough to heat tissue and cause damage. Non-ionizing radiation includes such electromagnetic frequencies as visible sunlight, invisible ultraviolet radiation from the sun, microwaves, radar, television and radio waves, electricity in wires, and infrared energy from heat lamps.

Radionuclides

Humans have identified over 1,800 known radionuclides (radioactive substances). In the nuclear field, the persistence of a substance is usually given in terms of its half-life, the time it takes for its radioactive emissions to be reduced by half. Radionuclides have half-lives from milliseconds to billions of years.

Alpha particles — Relatively large, positively charged particles that can be stopped by a layer of skin or sheet of paper. They can cause harm once inside the body.

Beta particles — Fast moving electrons that are smaller than alpha particles. They can penetrate 1-2 centimetres of water or flesh, but can be stopped by a few millimetres of aluminium.

Gamma radiation — Electromagnetic waves with high energy. It takes thick lead, concrete, water or other barriers to stop them.

X rays — Electromagnetic waves with greater energy and penetrating power than light.

Neutrons — Particles with high penetrating power, that come from outer space, reactors and nuclear explosions. Neutrons can make things radioactive.

The particles and waves listed above, with exception of neutrons in some cases, do not make the materials they strike radioactive.

Radiation measurements

The Standard International (SI) system uses measurements called becquerel, gray and sievert. This is replacing the older system which used the terms curie, rad and rem.

A becquerel (Bq) represents the radioactivity of material and the number of disintegrations per second.

A gray (Gy) is the dose of energy received from the radioactive material.

A sievert (Sv) is a measure of the potential biological damage cause by exposure to radiation.

Small radiation doses are recorded as millisieverts (mSv). The average Canadian's annual dose of natural radiation from the sun, rocks, food and the atmosphere has been estimated at 1 to 2 mSv. The average person gets an additional 0.34 to 1.7 mSv from such human-produced sources of radiation as building materials, glass, ceramics, water, food, tobacco, fuels, airport scanners and medical x-rays.

Danger limits for exposure to radiation

10 sieverts (10,000 mSv) or more of intense radiation in a single dose would destroy enough cells to be fatal.

1 S (1,000 mSv) in a single dose causes nausea and may cause cancer in 1 of 100 cases.

100 mSv has no observable effect when given instantly in a single dose.

Recommendations for exposure to radiation

The International Commission for Radiological Protection recommended in 1990 that members of the public not be exposed to more than 1 mSv a year of radiation from human-caused sources. The recommended maximum dose for radiation workers is 50 mSv a year, with a total dose of no more than 100 mSv over five years. The higher level for workers is set on the basis that it is voluntary, and the workers are compensated financially for the additional risk.

For comparison to older scales of measurement, 1 millisievert = 100 millirems.

People who live in certain areas are exposed to radon gas that is given off by natural radioactive materials in the ground. Radon enters houses, usually through cracks, floor drains or other openings in the basement. This slightly radioactive gas can be trapped inside the house and, if breathed in, can increase the risk of lung cancer.

CONTACTS FOR THE NEWS MEDIA

The following is a short list of environmental contacts for the news media. For more listings of government, business and environmental organizations, see federal and provincial phone books and such sources as *The Green List: A Guide to Canadian*

Environmental Organizations and Agencies, published by the Canadian Environmental Network.

FEDERAL GOVERNMENT

ENVIRONMENT CANADA

Environment Canada publishes a very extensive list of fact sheets, that are excellent references for a wide range of complex issues. In addition, a number of sections within Environment Canada can answer questions on specific issues.

Hugues Lacombe — Director General, Communications
10 Wellington Street
Hull, Québec K1A 0H3
Tel: (819) 997-6820 Fax: (819) 953-6789

General media inquiries:
Rod Giles — Public Affairs
10 Wellington Street
Hull, Québec K1A 0H3
Tel: (819) 953-6901 Fax: (819) 953-6789

ATMOSPHERIC ENVIRONMENT SERVICE :
Has material on acid rain, greenhouse effect, ozone layer and toxic chemicals in the air.

Nancy Bresolin — Director of Communications
LaSalle Academy, Block E, First Floor, 373 Sussex Drive
Ottawa, Ontario K1A 0H3
Tel: (613) 996-9270 Fax: (613) 943-1539

For information in Downsview (Toronto) offices also contact:
Heather Mackey — Senior Communications Officer
4905 Dufferin Street
Downsview, Ontario M3H 5T4
Tel: (416) 739-4759 Fax: (416) 739-4235

ECOSYSTEM SCIENCE AND EVALUATIONS DIRECTORATE

Has material on water quality and quantity, including water diversions.

Elizabeth Lefrançois — Head of water awareness and citizenship
10 Wellington St.
Hull, Québec K1A 0H3
Tel: (819) 953-6161 Fax: (819) 994-0237

PARKS CANADA

Deals with national parks and protected areas

Peter Serafini — Director of Communications
Jules Leger Building, 6th Floor,
25 Eddy Street
Hull, Québec K1A 0H3
Tel: (819) 997-3736 Fax: (819) 953-5523

CONSERVATION AND PROTECTION

Deals with pollution and wildlife issues

Patricia Dolan — Director of Communications
351 St. Joseph Boulevard
Hull, Québec K1A 0H3
Tel: (819) 997-6555 Fax: (819) 953-8125

ENVIRONMENTAL CHOICE PROGRAM

Information on products that are less environmentally damaging.

Michel Girard
107 Sparks Street, 2nd Floor
Ottawa, Ontario K1A 0H3
Tel: (613) 952-9440 Fax: (613) 952-9465

ENVIRONMENT CANADA REGIONALCOMMUNICATIONS
DIRECTORS

ATLANTIC REGION

Wayne Eliuk
45 Alderney Drive, 8th Floor
Dartmouth, Nova Scotia B2Y 2N6
Tel: (902) 426-1930 Fax: (902) 426-2690

RÉGION DE QUÉBEC
Clément Dugas
3, rue Buade, C.P. 6060 Haute-Ville
Québec, Québec J1R 4V7
Tel: (418) 648-7211 Fax: (418) 649-6140
ONTARIO REGION
Tamara Boughen
25 St. Clair Avenue East, 6th Floor
Toronto, Ontario M4T 1M2
Tel: (416) 973-1093 Fax: (416) 954-2262

CENTRAL REGION
Tim Hibbard
P.O. Box 22
Winnipeg, Manitoba R3C 0J7
Tel: (204) 983-2021 Fax: (204) 983-0964

WESTERN AND NORTHERN REGION
Sheila Watkins
Director of Communications
Twin Attria No. 2, 2nd Floor
Edmonton, Alberta T6B 2X3
Tel: (403) 468-8074 Fax: (403) 495-2615

PACIFIC AND YUKON REGION
Les Gallagher
Park Royal South, Kapilano 100, 3rd Floor
West Vancouver, British Columbia V7T 1A2
Tel: (604) 666-9733 Fax: (604) 666-4810

HEALTH AND WELFARE

This department provides advice to other departments, such as Environment Canada, and to other levels of government on the health impacts of chemicals, drugs, foods and medical equipment. It is an excellent source of information about the effects of toxic chemicals in the environment, and in food, air and drinking water. The Health Protection Branch publishes Issues sheets which provide excellent background on toxic substances and human health.

The media contact for health and environment issues is:

Monette Haché
Room 1926, Jeanne Mance Building
Tunney's Pasture
Ottawa, Ontario K1A OK9
Tel: (613) 957-1803   Fax: (613) 952-7747

GREAT LAKES HEALTH EFFECTS PROGRAM

Although the Great Lakes Health Effects Program seems to be regional in scope, its research into the health effects has national significance. The program can provide information on the implications of a number of toxic chemicals for health, particularly when those chemicals are in the food chain.

Room 136, Environmental Health Centre
Tunney's Pasture
Ottawa, Ontario K1A 0L2

Andrew Gilman, Manager
Tel: (613) 957-1876   Fax: (613) 952-9798

Mary Hegan, Communications,
Tel: (613) 952-8117   Fax: (613) 954-2486

AGRICULTURE CANADA

Responsible for setting regulations on pesticides, and for monitoring pesticide levels in Canadian food.

Janice Cansickle — Media Relations Unit
Communications Branch
Sir John Carling Building
930 Carling Avenue
Ottawa, Ontario K1A 0C5
Tel: (613) 995-8963   Fax: (613) 996-5911

Pesticides information call-line Ottawa. Tel: (613) 993-4544

ATOMIC ENERGY OF CANADA RESEARCH

Information on nuclear issues, safety, names of radioactive substances, nuclear power plants and related issues. Also does analyses of how pollutants, including chemicals, move in the environment.

John Perehinec — Media Relations
Chalk River Laboratories
Chalk River, Ontario K0J 1J0
Tel: (613) 584-3311, Ext. 4969   Fax: (613) 584-2227

FORESTRY CANADA

Has statistics on Canada's commercial forests and forest industry.

Francois Filion — Chief, Media, editing and ministerial services
21st Floor, Place Vincent Massey
351 St. Joseph Boulevard
Hull, Québec K1A OH3
Tel: (819) 997-1107   Fax: (819) 953-9646

ENERGY, MINES AND RESOURCES

Statistics on energy use and emissions leading to greenhouse effect.

Geneviève O'Sullivan — Director General of Communications
580 Booth Street, Room 856
Ottawa, Ontario K1A 0E4
Tel: (613) 996-3355   Fax: (613) 996-9094

FISHERIES AND OCEANS

Laws protecting fish from pollution. It is illegal under the Fisheries Act to destroy fish with pollution. The fisheries act is one of the strongest federal water pollution laws. There is a sustainable fisheries policy which says there is to be no net loss of fisheries habitat.

Cheryl Fraser — Director General
Habitat Management and Sustainable Development
200 Kent Street, 11th Floor
Ottawa, Ontario K1A 0E6
Tel: (613) 990-0007   Fax: (613) 993-7493

INDIAN AND NORTHERN AFFAIRS

Toxic chemicals in northerners, especially natives who eat wild food where toxic chemicals concentrate.

Becky Rynor — Media Relations
10 Wellington Street, Room 1901
Ottawa, Ontario K1A 0H4
Tel: (819) 997-8404   Fax: (819) 997-0268

TRANSPORT CANADA

Responsible for oil spill prevention and cleanup, and for control of foreign organisms in ballast water of ships visiting Canada. The zebra mussel, which has established itself in the Great Lakes, and could infiltrate waters in many parts of Canada, is just one example. This department is also responsible for vehicle mileage and pollution control.

Pierre Renart — Director, Intergovernmental and Environmental Affairs
Place de Ville, Tower C
Ottawa, Ontario K1A ON5
Tel: (613) 991-6503   Fax: (613) 991-6422

CANADIAN INTERNATIONAL DEVELOPMENT AGENCY

Canada's major source of funds for overseas projects. CIDA is putting considerable effort into making developing assistance environmentally sustainable.

Gabrielle Mathieu — Assistant Chief, Media Relations
Communications Branch
200 Promenade du Portage, 5th Floor
Hull, Québec K1A 0G4
Tel: (819) 953-9505   Fax: (819) 953-4933

INTERNATIONAL DEVELOPMENT RESEARCH CENTRE

This organization specializes in the training of people from other countries in a variety of skills. IDRC provides information on how various countries are dealing with environmental and development issues. IDRC maintains a clock which records the increase in global population and global land loss, a sobering reminder of how fast environmental pressures are growing.

Louise Behan, Diane Hardy — Media Relations Officer
P.O. Box 8500
Ottawa, Ontario K1G 3H9
Tel: (613) 236-6163, Ext. 2564   Fax: (613) 238-7230

PROVINCIAL GOVERNMENTS

The provinces have responsibility for most of the land and resources in Canada. The provinces have environmental expertise in such departments as environment, health, labor, natural resources, agriculture, energy and municipal affairs.

CANADIAN COUNCIL OF MINISTERS OF THE ENVIRONMENT

A co-ordinating group that can provide information on a number of issues in which the provinces, territories and the federal government are doing joint research or developing common policies.

Barbara Czech — Director of Communications
Canadian Council of Ministers of the Environment
326 Broadway, Suite 400
Winnipeg, Manitoba R3C 0S5
Tel: (204) 948-2130   Fax: (204) 948-2125

COMMUNICATIONS DIRECTORS FOR PROVINCES AND TERRITORIES

NEWFOUNDLAND

John Doody — Public Relations Specialist
Public Relations Group
Department of Environment and Lands
P.O. Box 8700
St. John's, Newfoundland A1B 4J6
Tel: (709) 729-0110   Fax: (709) 729-5645

NOVA SCOTIA

Margaret Murphy — Public Relations Officer
Department of Environment
P.O. Box 2107
HaliFax: Nova Scotia B3J 3B7
Tel: (902) 424-5300   Fax: (902) 424-0503

NEW BRUNSWICK

Gerry Hill — Director, Communications Branch
Department of Environment
P.O. Box 6000
Fredericton, New Brunswick E3B 5H1
Tel: (506) 453-3700   Fax: (506) 453-3843

PRINCE EDWARD ISLAND

Lea Bartley — Communications Officer
Department of the Environment
P.O. Box 2000
Charlottetown, Prince Edward Island C1A 7N8
Tel: (902) 368-5286   Fax: (902) 368-5830

QUEBEC

Louise Jacob — Directrice des communications
Ministère de l'environnement
3900, rue Marly
Sainte-Foy, Québec G1X 4E4
Tel: (418) 643-8807   Fax: (418) 643-3358

ONTARIO

Anne Boody — Director, Communications Branch
Ministry of the Environment
2nd floor, 135 St. Clair Avenue West
Toronto, Ontario M4V 1P5
Tel: (416) 323-4324   Fax: (416) 323-4643

MANITOBA

Paul White — Communications Coordinator
Department of Environment
3rd floor, 210 Osborne North
Winnipeg, Manitoba R3C 1B4
Tel: (204) 945-0750   Fax (204) 948-2147

SASKATCHEWAN

Harvey Linnen — Director of Public Affairs
Department of Environment and Public Safety
Room 218, 3085 Albert Street
Regina, Saskatchewan S4S 0B1
Tel: (306) 787-0740   Fax: (306) 787-0197

ALBERTA

Ellie Shuster — Director, Communications Division
Department of Environment
Main floor, 9820 - 106 Street
Edmonton, Alberta TK5 2JG
Tel: (403) 427-6267   Fax: (403) 422-3571

BRITISH COLUMBIA

Mark Stefanson — Director, Public Affairs and Communications
Ministry of Environment, Lands and Parks
810 Blanshard Street
Victoria, British Columbia V8V 1X5
Tel: (604) 387-9419   Fax: (604) 387-5703

YUKON

Mr. Pat Paslawski — Department of Renewable Resources
P.O. Box 2703
Whitehorse, Yukon Y1A 2C6
Tel: (403) 667-5237   Fax: (403) 667-3641

NORTHWEST TERRITORIES

Doug Stewart — Director, Conservation Education
Resource Development Division
Department of Renewable Resources
P.O. Box 1320
Yellowknife, Northwest Territories X1A 2L9
Tel: (403) 920-8716 Fax: (403) 873-0221 or 873-0114

PROVINCIAL WASTE MANAGEMENT AGENCIES

Several provinces have created organizations for dealing with hazardous industrial wastes.

ONTARIO WASTE MANAGEMENT CORPORATION

Tom Coleman — Director of Communications
2 Bloor Street West, 11th Floor
Toronto, Ontario M4W 3E2
Tel: (416) 923-2918 or 1-800-268-1178 Fax: (416) 923-7521

MANITOBA HAZARDOUS WASTE MANAGEMENT CORPORATION

Alun Richards — Manager, External Affairs
226-530 Century Street
Winnipeg, Manitoba R3H 0Y4
Tel: (204) 945-1844 Fax: (204) 945-5519

ALBERTA SPECIAL WASTE MANAGEMENT CORPORATION

Irene Chanin — Vice President, Communications
10909 Jasper Avenue, Suite 610
Edmonton, Alberta T5J 3L9
Tel: (403) 422-5029 Fax: (403) 482-9627

THE ALBERTA SPECIAL WASTE MANAGEMENT CENTRE

Canada's only permanent toxic chemical incinerator licensed to regularly burn high-level PCBs, as of 1992.
P.O. Box 180
Swan Hills, Alberta T0G 2C0

MUNICIPAL GOVERNMENTS

Municipal governments have a great amount of control over water, sewage, garbage and the development of land. The works department is usually in charge of water, sewer and garbage, and parks departments deal with such issues as trees and pesticide use in parks. A number of communities have round tables on environment and economy, or are part of a loose sustainable communities network. Some have specialized offices dealing with environmental protection issues. Following are the names of three broad municipal organizations involved in environmental issues:

INTERGOVERNMENTAL COMMITTEE ON URBAN AND
REGIONAL RESEARCH

Michel Gauvin — Executive Director
150 Eglinton Avenue East, Suite 301
Toronto, Ontario M4P 1E8
Tel: (416) 973-5629 Fax: (416) 973-1375

INTERNATIONAL COUNCIL FOR LOCAL ENVIRONMENTAL
INITIATIVES

Jeb Brugmann — Secretary General
City Hall, East Tower, 8th Floor
Toronto, Ontario M5H 2N2
Tel: (416) 392-1462 Fax: (416) 392-1478

CANADIAN URBAN INSTITUTE

Phil Ferguson — Program Director
City Hall, West Tower, 2nd Floor
Toronto, Ontario M5H 2N1
Tel: (416) 392-9171 Fax: (416) 392-4583

BUSINESS

A growing number of businesses are publishing annual environmental performance reports, listing their environmental impacts, and stating plans for reductions in those impacts. Some of the business and industrial organizations with information about environmental issues include:

BUSINESS COUNCIL ON NATIONAL ISSUES

Represents 150 of Canada's major corporations.

Heidi Hutchings — Communications Assistant
90 Sparks Street, Suite 806,
Ottawa, Ontario K1P 5B4
Tel: (613) 238-3727 Fax: (613) 236-8679

CANADIAN CHAMBER OF COMMERCE

Deals mainly with small and medium-sized business. Has 170,000 members across the country.

Roger Stanion — Senior Vice-President, Communications
55 Metcalfe Street
Ottawa, Ontario K1P 6N4
Tel: (613) 238-4000 Fax: (613) 238-7643

CANADIAN CHEMICAL PRODUCERS' ASSOCIATION

Information on chemicals, the Responsible Care program, and the National Emissions Reduction Masterplan (NERM).

Christine Gaynor — Public Affairs Advisor
350 Sparks Street, Suite 805
Ottawa, Ontario K1R 7S8
Tel: (613) 237-6215 Fax: (613) 237-4061

CANADIAN MANUFACTURERS' ASSOCIATION

Information on scope and scale of manufacturing in Canada. Has environmental committee.

Greg MacDonald — Director, Public Affairs
1 Yonge Street
Toronto, Ontario M5E 1J9
Tel: (416) 363-7261 Fax: (416) 363-3779

CANADIAN ASSOCIATION OF PETROLEUM PRODUCERS

Information on primary production of oil and gas.

Ann Beattie — Vice-President, Public Affairs
350-7th Avenue SW, Suite 2100
Calgary, Alberta T2P 3N9
Tel: (403) 267-1100 Fax: (403) 261-4622

CANADIAN PETROLEUM PRODUCTS INSTITUTE

This is the national association of petroleum refiners and marketers. Information on refined products such as gasoline and lubricating oils, and on safe disposal of used motor oil.

Brendan Hawley — Director of Public Affairs
275 Slater Street
Ottawa, Ontario K1P 5H9
Tel: (613) 232-3709 Fax: (613) 236-4280

CANADIAN POLYSTYRENE RECYCLING ASSOCIATION

This organization was created to recycle used polystyrene products.

Michael G. Scott — President
5925 Airport Road, Suite 200
Mississauga, Ontario L4V 1W1
Tel: (416) 612-8290 Fax: (416) 612-8024

CANADIAN PULP AND PAPER ASSOCIATION

Provides information on a wide range of forestry issues, particularly on pulp and paper production techniques and their environmental impacts.

Louis Fortier — Director, Public Information
1155 Metcalfe Street
Montréal, Québec H3B 4T6
Tel: (514) 866-6621   Fax: (514) 866-3035

CHLORINE INSTITUTE

Information about uses and environmental impacts of chlorine.

2001 L Street NW
Washington, D.C. 20036 U.S.A.
Tel: (202) 775-2790

COUNCIL OF FOREST INDUSTRIES OF B.C.

Information about forestry in British Columbia and old-growth logging.

555 Burrard Street, Suite 1200
Vancouver, B.C. V7X 1S7
Tel: (604) 684-0211   Fax: (604) 687-4930

COUNCIL OF GREAT LAKES INDUSTRIES

Involves a number of industries that have an impact on the lakes.

Detroit Windsor Port Corporation Building
174 South Clark Street
Detroit, Michigan 48209 U.S.A.
Tel: (313) 841-6700   Fax: (313) 841-6705

ENVIRONMENT AND PLASTICS INSTITUTE OF CANADA

This group was formed to help deal with plastic waste disposal.

Bob Hamp — Communications and Public Affairs
1262 Don Mills Road, Suite 104
Don Mills, Ontario M3B 2W7
Tel: (416) 449-3444   Fax: (416) 449-5685

LAMBTON INDUSTRIAL SOCIETY

Information about environmental issues, pollution controls and trends in Canada's major centre of chemical and petro-chemical production.

T. Scott Munro — General Manager
265 Front Street North, Suite 111
Sarnia, Ontario N7T 7X1
Tel: (416) 332-2010   Fax: (519) 332-2015

MINING ASSOCIATION OF CANADA

Information and statistics on mining, smelting, refining and mining by-products.

Jacques Hudon — Vice-President, Communications
350 Sparks Street, Suite 1105
Ottawa, Ontario K1R 7S8
Tel: (613) 233-9391   Fax: (613) 233-8897

SOCIETY OF THE PLASTICS INDUSTRY OF CANADA

Information on plastics in the environment.

Michael Hyde
1262 Don Mills Road, Suite 104
Don Mills, Ontario M3B 2W7
Tel: (416) 449-3444   Fax: (416) 449-5685

ENVIRONMENT GROUPS

The following is a very abbreviated list from the more than 2,000 environmental groups in the country. For a more complete list of environmental groups, see *The Green List: A Guide to Canadian Environmental Organizations and Agencies*, published by the Canadian Environmental Network.

CANADIAN ENVIRONMENTAL NETWORK

P.O. Box 1289, Station B
Ottawa, Ontario K1P 5R3
Tel: (613) 563-2078   Fax: (613) 563-7236

CANADIAN ENVIRONMENTAL LAW ASSOCIATION
517 College Street, Suite 401
Toronto, Ontario M6G 4A2
Tel: (416) 960-2284 Fax: (416) 960-9392

CANADIAN ECOLOGY ADVOCATES
St. Lawrence issues, especially beluga whales and toxic chemicals.
Leone Pippard — President and Executive Director
20, rue de l'Eglise
St-Jean, Québec G0A 3W0
Tel: (418) 829-1145 Fax: (418) 829-1276

CANADIAN INSTITUTE FOR ENVIRONMENTAL LAW AND
POLICY
517 College Street, Suite 400
Toronto, Ontario M6G 4A2
Tel: (416) 923-3529 Fax: (416) 960-9392

CONSERVATION COUNCIL OF NEW BRUNSWICK
180 St. John Street
Fredericton, N.B. E3B 4A9
Tel: (506) 458-8747

CONSERVATION COUNCIL OF ONTARIO
Represents a wide variety of groups. Works on development of
conservation strategies and comments on environmental policies.
489 College Street, Suite 506
Toronto, Ontario M6G 1A5
Tel: (416) 969-9637 Fax: (416) 960-8053

ECOLOGY ACTION CENTRE

Specializes in recycling and wastes.

3115 Veith Street, 3rd Floor
Halifax, N.S. B3K 3G9
Tel: (902) 454-7828   Fax: (902) 454-4766

ECOLOGY NORTH

Box 2888
Yellowknife, N.W.T. X1A 2R2
Tel: (403) 873-6019

ENERGY PROBE

Specializes in energy and nuclear power.

Norman Rubin — Director of Nuclear Research
225 Brunswick Avenue
Toronto, Ontario M5S 2M6
Tel: (416) 978-7014 Fax: (416) 978-3824

ENVIRONMENT COUNCIL OF ALBERTA

8th Floor, Weber Centre,
5555 Calgary Trail Southbound NW
Edmonton, Alberta T6H 5P9
Tel: (204) 427-5792 Fax: (204) 427-0388

FRIENDS OF THE EARTH, OTTAWA

Specializes in ozone issues, recycling.

Suite 701, 251 Laurier Avenue West
Ottawa, Ontario K1P 5J6
Tel: (212) 230-3352

GREAT LAKES TOMORROW

Works on Great Lakes issues in general

Suite 403, 720 Bathurst Street
Toronto, Ontario M5S 2R2
Tel: (416) 536-9161 Fax: (416) 539-9787

GREAT LAKES UNITED INC.

A binational group that deals with Great Lakes issues.

State University College
Cassetty Hall, 1400 Elmwood Ave.
Buffalo, N.Y. 14222, U.S.A.
Tel: (716) 886-0142 Fax (716) 886-0303

GREENPEACE— NATIONAL OFFICE

One of the best-known environment groups, worldwide. Carries out demonstrations against pollution, and produces a large amount of background material. Greenpeace also has offices in other parts of Canada and overseas.
185 Spadina Avenue, Suite 600
Toronto, Ontario M5T 2C6
Tel: (416) 345-8408 Fax: (416) 345-8462

MANITOBA NATURALISTS SOCIETY

128 James Avenue, Suite 302
Winnipeg, Manitoba R3B 0N8
Tel: (204) 943-9029

OPERATION CLEAN NIAGARA

Monitors toxic chemicals issues in the Niagara area.

Margherita Howe
83 Gage Street
Niagara-on-the-Lake, Ontario L05 1J0
Tel: (416) 468-3328

POLLUTION PROBE FOUNDATION

Specializes in toxic chemicals, Great Lakes, recycling, pollution, health and sustainable development.

Janine Ferretti — Executive Director
12 Madison Avenue
Toronto, Ontario, M5R 2S1
Tel: (416) 926-1043   Fax: (416) 926-1601

PROBE INTERNATIONAL

Focuses on international aid and development issues, such as the environmental impacts of large dams.

Patricia Adams — Executive Director
225 Brunswick Avenue
Toronto, Ontario M53 2M6
Tel: (416) 978-7014

PRESERVATION OF AGRICULTURAL LANDS SOCIETY

Wants more controls on building on tender fruit land in Niagara peninsula of southern Ontario.

Gracia Janes
Tel: (416) 468-2841

RAWSON ACADEMY OF AQUATIC SCIENCE

Experts on a wide range of water issues across Canada.

1 Nicholas Street, Suite 404
Ottawa, Ontario K1N 7B7
Tel: (613) 563-2636   Fax: (613) 563-4758

RECYCLING COUNCIL OF ONTARIO

Experts on a wide range of waste and recycling issues.

489 College Street, Suite 504
Toronto, Ontario M5G 1A5
Tel: (416) 960-1025   Fax: (416) 960-8053
Ontario Recycling Information Service 960-0938

SASKATCHEWAN ENVIRONMENTAL SOCIETY
Box 1372
Saskatoon, Saskatchewan S7K 3N9
Tel: (306) 665-1915 Fax: (306) 665-2128

SIERRA CLUB OF CANADA
Elizabeth May — National Representative
1 Nicholas Street, Suite 420
Ottawa, Ontario K1N 7B7
Tel: (613) 233-1906 Fax: (613) 233-2292

SOCIÉTÉ POUR VAINCRE LA POLLUTION
Focuses on water and other environment issues.
Daniel Green — Co-president
C.P. 65, succursale Place d'Armes
Montréal, Québec H2Y 3E9
Tel: (514) 844-5477

STOP
Specializes in air and water quality and waste reduction.
Bruce Walker — Research director
716, Saint-Ferdinand
Montréal, Québec H4C 2T2
Tel: (514) 932-7267

TORONTO FOOD POLICY COUNCIL
Rod MacRae — Coordinator
277 Victoria Street, 6th Floor
Toronto, Ontario M5B 1W1
Tel: (416) 392-1107 Fax: (416) 392-6657

VALHALLA SOCIETY

Interested in forestry, wilderness and parks, energy conservation.

Colleen McCrory
Box 224
New Denver, B.C. VOG 1S0
Tel: (604) 358-7158   Fax: (604) 358-7900

WEST COAST ENVIRONMENTAL LAW ASSOCIATION

207 West Hastings Street
Vancouver, B.C. V6B 1H7
Tel: (604) 684-7378   Fax: (604) 684-1312

WESTERN CANADA WILDERNESS COMMITTEE— HEAD OFFICE

Land use, logging, wilderness and parks.
20 Water Street
Vancouver, B.C. V6B 1A4
Tel: (604) 683-8220   Fax: (604) 683-8229

WORLD WILDLIFE FUND CANADA

Specializes in wildlife, including toxic substances and wildlife, and a national wildlands strategy.

Pegi Dover — Vice-President, Communications
90 Eglinton Avenue East, Suite 504,
Toronto, Ontario M4P 2Z7
Tel: (416) 489-8800   Fax: (416) 489-3611

ROUND TABLES ON ENVIRONMENT AND ECONOMY

There are round tables in every province and territory. A number are developing sustainable development (conservation) strategies. In addition, there is a growing number of municipal round tables.

NATIONAL ROUND TABLE ON THE ENVIRONMENT AND THE ECONOMY

1 Nicholas Street, Suite 1500
Ottawa, Ontario K1N 7B7
Tel: (613) 992-7189   Fax: (613) 992-7385

NEWFOUNDLAND AND LABRADOR ROUND TABLE ON ENVIRONMENT AND ECONOMY

P.O. Box 8700
St. John's, Newfoundland A1B 4J6
Tel: (709) 729-0027   Fax: (709) 729-1930

NOVA SCOTIA ROUND TABLE ON ENVIRONMENT AND ECONOMY

P.O. Box 2107
Halifax, Nova Scotia B3J 3B7
Tel: (902) 424-6346   Fax: (902) 424-0501

NEW BRUNSWICK ROUND TABLE ON ENVIRONMENT AND ECONOMY

P.O. Box 6000
Fredericton, New Brunswick E3B 5H1
Tel: (506) 453-3703   Fax: (506) 453-3843

PRINCE EDWARD ISLAND ROUND TABLE ON ENVIRONMENT AND ECONOMY

P.O. Box 2000
Charlottetown, Prince Edward Island C1A 7N8
Tel: (902) 368-5274   Fax: (902) 368-5830

TABLE RONDE QUÉBÉCOISE SUR L'ENVIRONNEMENT ET
L'ÉCONOMIE

3900, rue Marly, 5e étage, boite 78
Sainte-Foy, Québec G1X 4E4
Tel: (418) 643-7860   Fax: (418) 643-7812

ONTARIO ROUND TABLE ON ENVIRONMENT AND ECONOMY

790 Bay Street, Suite 1003
Toronto, Ontario M7A 1Y7
Tel: (416) 327-2032   Fax: (416) 327-2197

MANITOBA ROUND TABLE ON ENVIRONMENT AND ECONOMY

Unit 305 - 155 Carlton Street
Winnipeg, Manitoba R3C 3H8
Tel: (204) 945-1124   Fax: (204) 945-0090

SASKATCHEWAN ROUND TABLE ON ENVIRONMENT AND
ECONOMY

218 - 3085 Albert Street
Regina, Saskatchewan S4S 0B1
Tel: (306) 787-1627   Fax: (306) 787-0197

ALBERTA ROUND TABLE ON ENVIRONMENT AND ECONOMY

Suite 400, 9925 - 109 Street
Edmonton, Alberta T5K 2J8
Tel: (403) 427-5792   Fax: (403) 427-0388

BRITISH COLUMBIA ROUND TABLE ON ENVIRONMENT AND
ECONOMY

Market Square, 560 Johnson Street, Suite 229
Victoria, British Columbia V8W 3C6
Tel: (604) 387-5422   Fax: (604) 356-9276

NORTHWEST TERRITORIES ROUND TABLE ON THE
ENVIRONMENT AND THE ECONOMY
P.O. Box 1320
Yellowknife, Northwest Territories X1A 2L9
Tel: (403) 920-3210   Fax: (403) 873-3297

YUKON COUNCIL ON THE ECONOMY AND THE ENVIRONMENT
P.O. Box 2703
Whitehorse, Yukon Y1A 2C6
Tel: (403) 667-5939   Fax: (403) 668-4936

LABOUR

Labour organizations are often directly involved in environmental
issues, particularly over workers' exposure to toxic substances and
cases in which there are tradeoffs between jobs and environmental
protection. Two of the organizations which have been involved in
such issues from a broad perspective are:

CANADIAN LABOUR CONGRESS
National Representative - Workplace health, safety and
environment
2841 Riverside Drive
Ottawa, Ontario K1V 8X7
Tel: (613) 521-3400   Fax: (613) 521-4655

UNITED STEELWORKERS OF AMERICA
Health, workplace safety and general environmental concerns.
600 The East Mall, Suite 401
Etobicoke, Ontario M9B 4B1
Tel: (416) 626-6332   Fax: (416) 626-7745

RESEARCH, SCIENTIFIC AND ACADEMIC GROUPS

This is a category which includes think tanks and research groups which have expertise in the environmental field.

CANADIAN CENTRE FOR OCCUPATIONAL HEALTH AND SAFETY

A major centre of expertise on chemicals with a series of data bases that can be searched for detailed information.

Anne Gravereaux — Director, Inquiries Service
250 Main Street East
Hamilton, Ontario L8N 1H6
(416) 572-4400 or 1-800-263-8466

CANADIAN FEDERATION OF BIOLOGICAL SCIENCES

This organization has published Science Sources, a guide for reporters seeking Canadian experts in biological and biomedical scientists. The federation represents 6,000 researchers in 17 specialty groups, ranging from anatomists to toxicologists to zoologists.

Clément Gauthier — Science Policy Officer
360 Booth Street
Ottawa, Ontario K14 7K4
Tel: [613] 234-9555   Fax: [613] 234-6667

CANADIAN NETWORK OF TOXICOLOGY CENTRES

These centres provide expertise on toxic substances and health impacts.

CENTRE FOR TOXICOLOGY, UNIVERSITY OF GUELPH

Keith Solomon — Acting Executive Director
645 Gordon Street
Guelph, Ontario N1G 1Y3
Tel: (519) 837-3320   Fax: (519) 837-3861

TOXICOLOGY RESEARCH CENTRE
H. B. Schiefer — Director
University of Saskatchewan
Saskatoon, Saskatchewan S7N 0W0
Tel: (306) 966-7441   Fax: (306) 931-1664

CENTRE INTERUNIVERSITAIRE DE RECHERCHE EN TOXICOLOGIE
Gabriel Plaa — Directeur
Faculté du Médicine, Université
C.P. 6128, succursale A
Montréal, Québec H3C 3Y7
Tel: (514) 343-7722   Fax: (514) 343-6120

LE CENTRE SAINT-LAURENT/THE ST. LAWRENCE CENTRE
Thérèse Drapeau — Communications
105, rue McGill, Suite 400
Montréal, Québec H2Y 2E7
Tel: (514) 283-2343   Fax: (514) 283-4423

ECOLOGICAL AGRICULTURE PROJECTS
Stuart Hill — Assistant Professor of entomology and Director of
Ecological Agriculture Projects
Box 191, Macdonald College, McGill University
21, 111 Lakeshore Road
Ste-Anne de Bellevue, Québec H9X 1C0
Tel: (514) 398-7909

GREAT LAKES POLLUTION PREVENTION CENTRE
Susan Storr — Communications Officer
265 North Front Street, Suite 112
Sarnia, Ontario N7T 7X1
Tel: (519) 337-3423 or 1-800-667-9790   Fax: (519) 337-3486

INSTITUTE FOR RESEARCH ON PUBLIC POLICY

Environment and Sustainable Development Program

David Runnalls — Director
275 Slater Street
Ottawa, Ontario K1P 5H9
Tel: (613) 238-2296   Fax: (613) 235-8237

INTERNATIONAL INSTITUTE FOR SUSTAINABLE DEVELOPMENT

Created by Federal and Manitoba governments to provide international research and leadership on sustainable development.

Bonnie Bisnett — Communications
212 McDermot Avenue
Winnipeg, Manitoba R3B 0S3
Tel: (204) 958-7700   Fax: (204) 958-7710

ROYAL SOCIETY OF CANADA, CANADIAN GLOBAL CHANGE PROGRAM

The Royal Society is Canada's major association of scientists. The Canadian Global Change Program promotes co-ordination of Canadian research on global change issues, and provides information on global change at a national and international levels.

Brian Bornhold — Program Director, Canadian Global Change Program
P.O. Box 9734
Ottawa, Ontario K1G 5J4
Tel: (613) 991-5639   Fax: (613) 991-6996

WATERLOO CENTRE FOR GROUNDWATER RESEARCH

An internationally-known centre of expertise on underground water issues.

University of Waterloo
Waterloo, Ontario N2L 3G1
Tel: (519) 885-1211, Ext. 2892   Fax: (519) 888-4654

There are also dozens of universities and community colleges in Canada where one can find experts on a wide range of environmental subjects. Contact the environment, forestry, chemistry or natural resource departments, or call the communications and public affairs department for the university or college. Many institutions publish lists of experts by subject.

FIRST NATIONS

ASSEMBLY OF FIRST NATIONS

Involved in treaty rights discussions.

Carole Mills — Co-ordinator, E.A.G.L.E. Project (Effects on Aboriginals from the Great Lakes Environment)
47 Clarence Street, Suite 300
Ottawa, Ontario K1N 9K1
Tel: (613) 236-0673   Fax: (613) 238-5780

CREE REGIONAL AUTHORITY

Involved in dispute over flooding of land for power dams in Québec.

Chief Matthew Coon-Come has been the major spokesperson.
2 Lakeshore Road
Nemasta, Québec J0Y 3B0
Tel: (819) 673-2600 or (613) 761-1655   Fax: (819) 673-2606

WALPOLE ISLAND HERITAGE CENTRE

Deals with pollution in St. Clair River and Lake St. Clair area from perspective of first nations.

Dean Jacobs — Executive Director
R.R. No. 3
Wallaceburg, Ontario N8A 4K9
Tel: (519) 627-1475   Fax: (416) 627-1530

INTERNATIONAL AND OVERSEAS ORGANIZATIONS

BUSINESS COUNCIL FOR SUSTAINABLE DEVELOPMENT

A high-level international group that provides co-ordination and information on sustainable development from a business perspective.

Hugh Faulkner — Executive Director
Case Postale 365
CH-1210 Geneva, Switzerland
Tel: (41 22) 788 32 02   Fax (41 22) 788 32 11

CENTRE FOR OUR COMMON FUTURE

This organization was created to carry on some of the work of the Brundtland Commission. It is a key centre of information on who is doing what about sustainable development around the world.

Warren Lindner — Executive Director
Palais Wilson, 52, rue des Pâquis
CH-1201 Geneva, Switzerland
Tel: (41 22) 732 71 17   Fax: (41 22) 738 50 46

GREAT LAKES FISHERY COMMISSION

This Canada-United States organization has two major roles:
To defuse fishery disputes between Canada and the United States or among state and provincial governments. and to control sea lamprey in the Great Lakes.

Robert Beecher — Executive Secretary
2100 Commonwealth Boulevard, Suite 209
Ann Arbor, Michigan 48105-1563 U.S.A.
Tel: (313) 662-3209   Fax: (313) 668-2531

INTERNATIONAL JOINT COMMISSION

A bi-national organization, appointed by the Prime Minister of Canada and President of the United States. The commission deals with boundary water quantity and quality issues between the two countries, especially Great Lakes issues. Does excellent reports on the state of the lakes, toxic chemicals, human and wildlife health.

CANADIAN SECTION
100 Metcalfe Street, 18th Floor
Ottawa, Ontario K1P 5M1
Tel: (613) 995-2984   Fax: (613) 993-5583

GREAT LAKES REGIONAL OFFICE
100 Ouellette Avenue, 8th Floor
Windsor, Ontario N9A 6T3.
Tel: (519) 256-7821   Fax: (519) 256-7791

POPULATION INSTITUTE

110 Maryland Avenue NE, Suite 207
Washington, D.C. 20002 U.S.A.
Tel: (202) 544-3300

UNITED NATIONS ENVIRONMENT PROGRAMME, NORTH AMERICAN OFFICE

The closest contact for information on UNEP, and for reports and contacts on major international environmental issues.

Janet Edwards — Information assistant
Room DC 2-803, Two United Nations Plaza
New York, N.Y. 10017 U.S.A.
Tel: (212) 963-8093   Fax: (212) 963-7341

UNITED NATIONS ENVIRONMENT PROGRAMME
HEADQUARTERS

Tore Brevik — Chief, Information and public affairs
P.O. Box 30552
Nairobi, Kenya (Time difference +8 hours with Toronto)
The executive director of UNEP is Elizabeth Dowdeswell, a former senior Environment Canada official.
Tel: (25 42) 333 930   Fax: (25 42) 520 302

THE UNITED NATIONS CONFERENCE ON ENVIRONMENT AND DEVELOPMENT

Secretariat has been succeeded by other UN organizations which are to carry on the work started at the Earth Summit in Rio de Janeiro in 1992.

DEPARTMENT FOR POLICY COORDINATION AND SUSTAINABLE DEVELOPMENT

Jean-Claude Faby
United Nations, Secretariat Building, Room S-3060
New York, N.Y. 10017 U.S.A.
Tel: (212) 963-5900   Fax: (212) 963-1010
Under this department, the Commission on Sustainable Development is being created.

DEPARTMENT OF PUBLIC INFORMATION

Room S-894, United Nations
New York, N.Y. 10017 U.S.A
Julie Thompson, Tel: (212) 963-4295,
or
Pragati Pascale, Tel: (212) 963-6870
Fax: (212) 963-4556

UNITED NATIONS POPULATION FUND

This is a good source of information on global population trends.

Hiro Ando — Chief, Information and External Relations Division
220 East 42nd Street
New York, N.Y. 10017 U.S.A.
Tel: (212) 297-5020   Fax: (212) 557-6416

UNITED NATIONS DEVELOPMENT PROGRAMME

This organization has excellent information on such issues as the disparity in income among nations.

Soren Dyssegaard — Director of Public Affairs
One United Nations Plaza
New York, NY 10017 U.S.A.
Tel: (212) 906-5300

WARMER BULLETIN

An excellent source of information on waste issues.
83 Mount Ephraim
Tunbridge Wells, Kent TN4 8BS, England
Tel: (44 892) 524626   Fax: (44 892) 525287

WORLD CONSERVATION UNION

Information on the World Conservation Strategy, wildlife, wildlands and sustainable development.

Rue Mauverney 28
CH-1196, Gland, Switzerland
Tel: (41 22) 64 91 14   Fax: (41 22) 64 29 26

WORLD WIDE FUND FOR NATURE

Wilderness and wildlife issues.
Avenue du Mont Blanc
CH-1196 Gland, Switzerland
Tel: (41 22) 64 91 11   Fax: (41 22) 64 32 39

WORLDWATCH INSTITUTE

An excellent source of international environmental information. Publishes annual State of the World report, issue papers and Worldwatch Magazine.
1776 Massachusetts Avenue NW
Washington, D.C. 20036, U.S.A.
Tel: (202) 452-1999   Fax: (202) 296-7365

WORLD RESOURCES INSTITUTE

An excellent source of international environmental information. Publishes a major world environmental data report biennially, as well as separate papers on issues.

1709 New York Avenue NW
Washington, D.C. 20006 U.S.A
Tel: (202) 638-6300   Fax: (202) 638-0036

ZERO POPULATION GROWTH

Information on population issues from an independent organization.

1400 16th Street NW, Suite 230
Washington, D.C. 20036 U.S.A.
Tel: (202) 332-2200   Fax: (202) 332-2302

MEDIA ORGANIZATIONS

CANADIAN ASSOCIATION OF JOURNALISTS

Not specialized in environment, but holds some seminars on environmental issues.

Carleton University, St. Patrick's Building
Ottawa, Ontario K1S 5B6
Tel: (613) 788-7424   Fax: (613) 788-5604

CANADIAN SCIENCE WRITERS' ASSOCIATION

Not specialized in environment, but holds some seminars on environmental issues.

24 Ryerson Avenue, Suite 303
Toronto, Ontario M5T 2P3
Tel: (416) 361-1427   Fax: (416) 860-0826

SOCIETY OF ENVIRONMENTAL JOURNALISTS

Has U.S. and Canadian members. Publishes a very useful newsletter on environmental reporting.

Amy Gahran — SEJ Records Manager
7904 Germantown Avenue
Philadelphia, PA 19118
Tel: (215) 630-9147

SCIENTISTS' INSTITUTE FOR PUBLIC INFORMATION

Refers journalists to qualified sources of information on science and environmental issues for interviews. Also provides addresses for videotape clips on issues.

Roshi Pelaseyed — 355 Lexington Avenue
New York, N.Y. 10017
Director, Global Change Program
Tel: (212) 661-9110   Fax: (212) 599-6432

SOURCES: THE DIRECTORY OF CONTACTS FOR EDITORS, REPORTERS AND RESEARCHERS

Not specialized in environment, but provides broad list of contact names on a wide range of issues. Journalists receive this free, and it is sold to other users.

Barrie Zwicker — Publisher and Editor
4 Phipps Street, Suite 109
Toronto, Ontario M4Y 1J5
Tel: (416) 964-7799   Fax: (416) 964-8763

A SHORT HISTORY OF THE ENVIRONMENT

1885
Canada creates a federal reserve that will become Banff National Park, the nation's first national park.

1909
The United States and Great Britain, on behalf of Canada, sign the Boundary Waters Treaty. Its main role is to help to settle disputes on the sharing of boundary waters, and it presaged growing concerns about pollution with the phrase: "Boundary waters and waters flowing across the boundary shall not be polluted on either side to the injury of health or property on the other." Under the treaty, the International Joint Commission is created to monitor and adjudicate on boundary water issues.

1915
Canada's Commission on Conservation wrote about the need to live within natural cycles by saying: "Each generation is entitled to the interest on the natural capital, but the principal should be handed on unimpaired." This presages modern discussions about sustainable development.

1941
A ruling in the Trail Smelter Case says that: "No state has the right to use or permit the use of its territory in such a manner as to cause injury by fumes in or to the territory of another, or to the persons or property therein, when the case is of serious consequence and the injury is established by clear and convincing evidence." In this case, air pollution from a Canadian lead-zinc smelter in Trail, B.C. was damaging orchards and crops in Washington state.

The 1950s
Atmospheric nuclear testing releases radioactive iodine and strontium 90 into air, and fallout gets into milk in the Northeren Hemisphere.

1952
During the killer smog in London, England more than 4,000 people die from heart and lung disease, and the rate of respiratory illness doubled.

1956

Widespread mercury poisoning discovered in the Japanese fishing village of Minamata. Mercury dumped by a chemical plant got into fish and shellfish, killing and causing injury to several hundred people.

1962

Rachel Carson published *Silent Spring*, which launched the modern era of concern about the harmful effects of pesticides, such as DDT, in the environment.

1963

A treaty is signed by a number of nations, banning the atmospheric testing of nuclear weapons.

1968

Cooking oil in Yusho, Japan contaminated with PCBs, furans and polychlorinated quaterphenyls gets into rice, and people develop chloracne, sensory changes and other ailments.

1970

Dangerous levels of mercury found in fish in several parts of Ontario, causing fishery closures. This awakens Canadians to the dangers of chemicals in the aquatic food chain.

The first Earth Day is held in the United States.

1971

Canada establishes a federal environment department.

1972

The Stockholm Conference on the Human Environment, headed by Canadian Maurice Strong, focuses attention on global environmental issues, and leads to creation of a United Nations Environment Programme, and the formation of many environment departments around the world.

Canada and the United States sign first Great Lakes Water Quality Agreement, committing the two nations to control sewage and phosphorus discharges.

The Club of Rome publishes *The Limits to Growth*. Although many of its calculations about the world running out of natural resources by specific dates were inaccurate, it made people think about the concept of limiting some forms of development.

1973
The Science Council of Canada added another term to our lexicon with the phrase, "conserver society." It said that, "Canadians, as individuals, and their governments, institutions and industries, (must) begin the transition from a consumer society preoccupied with resource exploitation, to a conserver society engaged in more constructive endeavours."

1974
Scientists said that chlorine released into the atmosphere in CFCs would damage the ozone layer.

1978
Canada and United States sign the second Great Lakes Water Quality Agreement. This agreement introduced the concept of protecting the entire ecosystem of the lakes, the philosophy of zero discharge of persistent toxic substances to the lakes, and the policy of the virtual elimination of inputs of persistent toxic substances.

The United States raises concerns that Canada may be about to pollute the United States with acid rain.

The Love Canal toxic waste dump in Niagara Falls, New York becomes an international symbol of hazardous wastes. Part of the neighborhood is declared a disaster area, and the first of 850 families are evacuated.

1979
The Three Mile Island nuclear power plant in Pennsylvania experiences a near-meltdown of its reactor core.

Canada and United States sign memorandum of intent to negotiate a clean air agreement to curb acid rain.

In the world's largest environmental evacuation, 225,000 people flee their homes in Mississauga, west of Toronto, when a train with tank cars of propane and chlorine crashes, and the subsequent fire releases poisonous chlorine gas.

1980
A World Conservation Strategy is published by the International Union for the Conservation of Nature, the United Nations Environment Programme and the World Wildlife Fund, and warns that humans must protect nature in their own self-interest.

Dioxin (2,3,7,8-TCDD), the most toxic synthetic substance, is reported in Lake Ontario herring gulls.

1983
United Nations votes to create the World Commission on Environment and Development.

1984
Seven eastern provinces agree to cut acidic sulphur dioxide emissions by half by 1994.

In Bhopal, India, a leak of methyl isocyanate, a lethal gas used in making insecticides, from a Union Carbide Corp. pesticide plant killed more than 3,000 people and injured about 75,000.

1985
Hole in the Antarctic ozone layer discovered. It had existed for a decade, but satellite data indicating the problem had been discarded as unreliable.

Spill of PCBs on a highway near Kenora, and spill of perchloroethylene dry cleaning fluid into the St. Clair River at Sarnia raise questions about the control of hazardous chemicals.

1986
Explosion and fire in reactor 4 at Chernobyl in Ukraine. Officials said about seven tonnes of radioactive material escaped into the atmosphere. Radiation circles world in 11 days, and fallout contaminates food in parts of Europe.

Following visit of Brundtland Commission, Canada's environment ministers create the National Task Force on Environment and

Economy. It includes environment ministers, business leaders and environmentalists.

1987

Release of the Brundtland Report *Our Common Future*, by the World Commission on Environment and Development.

Canada's National Task Force on Environment and Economy releases its report on what Canada needs to do to move toward sustainable development.

Signing of Montreal Protocol to control substances that deplete the ozone layer.

Canada and the United States sign a protocol to strengthen the Great Lakes Water Quality Agreement, and another agreement to reduce Niagara River pollution.

1988

While droughts cause hardship in western North America and the Mississippi River drops to lowest recorded levels, the Toronto Atmosphere Conference calls for at least a 50 per cent cut in global carbon dioxide emissions to stop climate warming.

A fire in a warehouse containing PCBs at St. Basile-le-Grand, near Montreal, causes evacuation of over 3,300 people for three weeks.

Canada begins to create Round Tables on Environment and Economy, as recommended by National Task Force on Environment and Economy.

1989

116 nations meeting in Basel, Switzerland approve a convention which requires that waste be exported only to those countries which are equipped to safely handle them. This came after the dumping of hazardous wastes in poor African and Caribbean nations.

The oil tanker Exxon Valdez spills 270,000 barrels of Alaska crude when it hits a reef in Prince William Sound, just out of the Alaskan port of Valdez, causing North America's largest oil spill.

Cod fishing quotas are severely reduced in Atlantic because of over fishing. Plants shut down and people laid off.

1990

Hagersville Tire Fire in southern Ontario. Youths start a fire in a pile of 14 million tires. It cost about $1.5 million to put out fire. Provokes debate over whether to burn Ontario's 28 million waste tires a year in cement kilns as fuel or to try to recycle them. A tire fire at St-Amable, just east of Montreal burns later the same year.

London Amendment to the Montreal Protocol advances dates for elimination of CFCs. Fund created to help poorer nations switch to ozone friendly products.

United States amends Clean Air Act to impose new controls on acid gases.

Federal Green Plan released. The largest environmental plan in Canadian history, promises $3 billion in new funding over 6 years. Includes plans for smog controls, reduction in toxic wastes, safer drinking water and more national parks.

1991

Persian Gulf War begins and Allied forces attack Iraq over its occupation of Kuwait. Huge oil spill fouls the Persian Gulf. Iraq sets fire to hundreds of Kuwaiti oil wells, blanketing the region in smoke, and causing fallout of soot as far away as the Himalayas.

The Canada-United States Air Quality Accord marks the end of a decade of negotiations over a pact to reduce transboundary flows of acid gas emissions from both countries. Up to half the acid fallout in eastern Canada was blamed on U.S. sources.

Federal government releases new pulp and paper regulations that say mills must not release measurable amounts of dioxins and furans by 1994.

1992

Warnings that the ozone layer over Canada is at risk leads the federal government to announce a UV index to alert Canadians to the risk of too much sunlight.

The Earth Summit, the United Nations Conference on Environment and Development, was held in Rio de Janeiro, Brazil. The conference, headed by Canadian Maurice Strong, was the largest meeting of world leaders in history. The major document from Rio was Agenda 21, a blueprint on how to make development socially, economically and environmentally sustainable. The conference began the signing of agreements on greenhouse gas emisions and the protection of biological diversity. It also produced a declaration on the environmental rights of responsibilities of nations, and a statement of principles on the use and protection of forests.

Canadian government imposes major cuts on east coast fisheries in an effort to prevent a collapse of various fish stocks. Thousands of people are put out of work.

An agreement signed in Copenhagen advances target date for the elimination of new CFC uses to the end of 1995.

GLOSSARY

(Much of this material has been adapted from the Glossary of Selected Terms of *The State of Canada's Environment— 1991* and from the Glossary of *A Vital Link: Health and the Environment in Canada*.)

Acceptable daily intake — The intake from all sources of a given substance that appears to be without appreciable risk, even if taken in at this level for a lifetime.

Acid rain — More correctly known as acid precipitation, because it includes rain, snow, sleet, fog, mist and dry particles. It is the result of emissions of sulphur and nitrogen oxides, that produce sulphuric and nitric acids when in contact with water, particularly in the presence of sunlight in the atmosphere.

Acute toxicity — Capable of causing severe harm or death in relatively short periods time.

Acutely lethal effluent — Discharges that kill half the fish (usually rainbow trout) exposed to it for 96 hours (four days).

Anadromous — Species of fish, such as salmon, that migrate from the oceans to fresh water to breed.

Anaerobic — Bodies of water can become anaerobic (devoid of oxygen) when pollution feeds the growth of bacteria, which use up the available dissolved oxygen in the water. This leads to "dead zones" on the bottom of lakes.

Adsorbable Organic Halogen (AOX) — A measure of the total organic chlorine concentration in effluent. This is often used as an indicator of the level of contamination by organic chemicals.

Aquifer — An underground geological formation in which water lies between rocks, gravel, sand or other porous material.

Atmosphere — The envelope of gases surrounding the earth and held to it by gravitational attraction.

Background radiation — Naturally occurring radiation from cosmic rays, radon from natural radioactive materials in the soil and, in some cases, refers to fallout from nuclear weapons tests.

Benthos — Plant and animal life that lives on the bottom of water bodies.

Bioaccumulation — The process in which chemicals become more concentrated the higher they are located in the food chain. This happens when the intake of a substance is greater than the rate at which it is excreted or metabolized.

Biochemical oxygen demand (BOD) — The total demand for oxygen by living creatures in an aquatic system. BOD refers to the amount of dissolved oxygen in water that will be used by bacteria to decompose organic waste. If that oxygen demand is too high, fish and other aquatic life are deprived of oxygen they need to live.

Biodegradable — Capable of being broken down into simple compounds by living organisms, especially bacteria.

Biomass — An ecological term referring to the dry weight of all organic matter in a given ecosystem. In energy stories, it refers to plant material or animal wastes that can be burned as fuel.

Biosphere — The regions of the planet where life is found, ranging from the oceans to the lower atmosphere.

Biota — Living creatures, including plants, animals and micro-organisms.

Cancer — An uncontrolled growth of cells that can invade and destroy body organs.

Carcinogen — A cancer-causing agent.

Carrying capacity — The amount of life and exploitation that a biological system can support without suffering damage and becoming degraded.

149

Chlorination — In the case of drinking water or sewage treatment, this refers to the process of adding chlorine to water to disinfect it.

Chlorofluorocarbons — A class of chemical compounds, also known as CFCs, that contain carbon, fluorine and chlorine, and are damaging the ozone layer.

Chronic or sub-lethal effects — Harmful effects that do not result in the immediate death of organisms, but cause adverse effects after long-term exposure.

Coliform — Bacteria normally found in the intestines of animals and humans. In water, they indicate pollution from human or animal wastes, and are capable of causing illness.

DNA — Deoxyribonucleic acid, which is found in the nucleus of cells, carries the genetic codes that instruct living organisms how to develop and function.

Desertification — The spreading of deserts, which are areas of low biological productivity, as a result of human or natural processes. Humans cause desertification, which means a loss of the productivity of land, through deforestation, soil erosion, waterlogging, salinization, and other processes of soil degradation.

Dissolved oxygen — Tiny oxygen bubbles in the water, which are used by aquatic organisms.

Ecosphere — The global ecosystem, including atmosphere, soil, water and living organisms.

Ecosystem — A defined region (large or small) including all its living organisms. Generally seen as a region in which living organisms have a relatively stable relationship.

Ecosystem approach — An approach that takes account of all the impacts and interactions of an activity on the environment.

Effluent — Liquid waste that is discharged into the environment.

Eutrophication — Over fertilization of a water body by nutrients that produce more plant matter (usually algae) than the water body and its other living organisms can absorb. This can happen naturally, over a long time, or can be caused rapidly by human discharges of large amounts of fertilizers, such as phosphorus.

Gas chromatograph, mass spectrometer (GCMS) — A device that is used to measure the level of substances in environmental samples. The concentrations of pollutants are often given in parts per million, per billion or per trillion.

Greenhouse effect — Gases such as water vapour and carbon dioxide create a natural greenhouse effect on earth because they maintain a global average temperature of about 15 degrees Celsius. Human releases of gases such as carbon dioxide, nitrous oxide, methane and chlorofluorocarbons, are predicted to increase the greenhouse effect in a process known as climate warming.

Ground water — The technical term used for underground water supplies, including those that can be tapped by wells.

Half-life — The period in which a given amount of pollution decreases by half in the environment. In radiation, the time for half the radiological activity to cease.

Heavy metals — These include such toxic metals as mercury, lead and cadmium, that are biologically harmful, even in very small doses.

Hydrogeology — The science of determining underground water movements.

Leachate — The contaminated runoff from dumps. Generally the concern is about toxic chemicals that are being carried out of dumps by water.

LRTAP — Long-Range Transport of Air Pollutants or Long-Range Transport of Acidic Precipitation.

Non-point source pollution — Pollution that comes from diffuse sources, such as runoff from land. This includes bacteria, pesticides, fertilizers and other chemicals and wastes, that are carried into watercourses by rainwater and melting snow.

Mutagen — This is a substance or effect that changes genetic material, and when cells divide, the changes are passed along, through generations.

Organic — Containing hydrogen. Often used to mean plant or animal material. Organic food generally means it has not been treated with synthetic chemicals.

Ozone — A gas made up of three atoms of oxygen. It occurs naturally in the stratosphere, and is produced by pollution at ground level. It is also manufactured to sterilize such products as drinking water.

Pelagic — Organisms that swim or drift in water, and do not live on the bottom.

Pesticides — Substances that are used to kill unwanted plants, insects, animals and other living creatures.

Photodegradable — Capable of being broken down by the action of sunlight.

Point source pollution — Pollution that comes from clearly identifiable sources, such as discharge pipes from industries and municipalities.

Pollution — Levels of any substance that cause harm to human health or natural systems.

Radiation — The emission or transmission of energy in the form of electromagnetic waves or particles. It includes radio waves, solar radiation, and the products of nuclear medicine, reactors and weapons.

Radioisotopes — Elements that are radioactive, whether naturally, such as uranium, or those that are produced deliberately for medicine, industrial, power generation or military use.

Radon — An invisible, naturally occurring radioactive gas. It becomes an environmental problem when it seeps from natural sources in the ground into homes, where it can be inhaled. Its decay products, known as daughters of radon, can cause lung cancer.

Sludge — Liquid waste that is in a semi-solid form. It comes from municipal sewage treatment plants and from some industries.

Tailings — Mining wastes from which minerals have been extracted. Tailings contain ground-up rock and metals, and may contain salts, sulphur compounds and radioactive material that can leach into watercourses.

Teratogen — An agent that alters the formation of cells, tissue and organs, causing changes in the fetus during development and resulting in birth defects.

Threshold limit value — The TLV is the concentration of pollution in air to which most workers can be exposed daily on the basis that this will not cause harm.

Total suspended solids — Fine particles of solid matter, such as wood fibre or dirt found in water. TSS can smother the breeding grounds of fish by carpeting the bottom of lakes and rivers.

Volatile organic compounds — VOCs are organic gases and vapors that are considered an air pollutant. They come from sources including the burning of fuels, the use of paints and solvents, and dry cleaning operations.

Wetland — Includes marsh, swamp, bog, fen, pond, reed swamp, carr, peat bog, wetland meadow, wetland forest and thicket. The area where land meets water, and where productivity of life is very high. Technically, a place where the water table is at or above the ground level, but may drop below the surface during dry seasons. Usually limited to waters two metres deep.

READING LIST

BOOKS

Allen, Robert, *How to Save the World, a Strategy for World Conservation*, Kogan Page, London, 1981.

Attenborough, David, *Life on Earth*, Little Brown, Toronto, 1979.

Bocking, Richard C., *Canada's Water: For Sale?* James Lewis and Samuel, Toronto, 1972.

Bourassa, Robert, *Power from the North*, Prentice-Hall, Scarborough, 1985.

Brown, Lester et al, Worldwatch Institute, *State of the World*, Norton, Washington (published annually).

Canadian Council of Resource and Environment Ministers, *Report of the National Task Force on Environment and Economy*, Downsview, 1987.

Canadian Environmental Network, *The Green List: A Guide to Canadian Environmental Organizations and Agencies*, Ottawa, 1991.

Carson, Rachel, *Silent Spring*, Fawcett Crest, New York, 1962.

Commission on Developing Countries and Global Change, *For Earth's Sake,* International Development Research Centre, Ottawa, 1992.

Energy Options Advisory Committee, *Energy and Canadians into the 21st Century*, Energy, Mines and Resources Canada, Ottawa, 1988.

Environment Canada, *Conference Statement, The Changing Atmosphere: Implications for Global Security,* Ottawa, 1988.

Friedman, Sharon and Kenneth, *Reporting on the Environment: A Handbook for Journalists*, Department of Journalism and Communication, Lehigh University, Bethlehem, Pennsylvania, 1988.

Government of Canada, *Canada's Green Plan*, Minister of Supply and Services Canada, Ottawa, 1990.

Government of Canada, *Toxic Chemicals in the Great Lakes and Associated Effects,* Environment Canada, Department of Fisheries and Oceans, Health and Welfare, 1991.

Government of Canada, *The State of Canada's Environment — 1991*, Ottawa, 1991.

Health and Welfare Canada, *A Vital Link: Health and the Environment in Canada,* Ottawa, 1992.

Hummel, Monte, *Endangered Spaces: The Future for Canada's Wilderness*, Key Porter Books, Toronto, 1989.

Keating, Michael, *To The Last Drop*, Macmillan of Canada, Toronto, 1986.

Keating, Michael, *Toward a Common Future,* Environment Canada, Ottawa, 1989.

Keating, Michael, *The Earth Summit's Agenda for Change,* Center for Our Common Future, Geneva, 1993.

Kruus, Peter et al, *Chemicals in the Environment,* Polyscience Publications Inc., Morin Heights, 1991.

LaMay, Craig L., and Dennis, Everette E., *Media and the Environment,* Freedom Forum Media Studies Center, Island Press, Washington, 1991.

Lewis, R.J., *Hazardous Chemicals Desk Reference, 2nd Edition*, Van Nostrand Reinhold, New York, 1991.

MacNeill, Jim, Winsemius, Pieter and Yakushiji, Taizo, *Beyond Interdependence: The Meshing of the World's Economy and the Earth's Ecology,* Oxford, New York, 1991.

Meadows, Donella, et al, *The Limits to Growth,* Signet, New York, 1972.

Mungall, Constance and McLaren, Digby, (editors), *Planet Under Stress: The Challenge of Global Change,* The Royal Society of Canada, Oxford, 1990.

Munroe, Glenn, *Profit from Pollution Prevention: A Guide to Waste Reduction and Recycling in Canada,* Pollution Probe Foundation, Toronto, 1990.

Myers, Norman (general editor), *Gaia, An Atlas of Planet Management,* Anchor/Doubleday, Garden City, N.Y., 1984.

Paehlke, Robert C., *Environmentalism and the Future of Progressive Politics,* Yale University Press, New Haven, 1989.

Pearse, Peter H., MacLaren, James W. and Bertrand, Françoise, *Currents of Change, Final Report of the Inquiry on Federal Water Policy,* Environment Canada, Ottawa, 1985.

Schumaker, E.F., *Small is Beautiful: Economics as if People Mattered,* Harper and Row, New York, 1973.

Science Council of Canada, *Water 2020, Sustainable Use for Water in the 21st Century,* Report 40, Ottawa, 1988.

Science Council of Canada, *Environmental Peacekeepers: Science, Technology and Sustainable Development in Canada,* Ottawa, 1988.

Sittig, M., *Handbook of Toxic and Hazardous Chemicals and Carcinogens,* Noyes Publishing, 1985.

Starke, Linda, *Signs of Hope: Working Towards Our Common Future,* The Centre for Our Common Future, Oxford, New York, 1990.

Tolba, Mostafa K., *Saving Our Planet: Challenges and Hopes, The State of the Environment (1972-1992),* Chapman and Hall, London, 1992.

Postel, Sandra, Worldwatch Institute, *Last Oasis: Facing Water Scarcity,* Norton, New York, 1992.

United Nations Environment Programme and World Wide Fund for Nature, *Caring for the Earth: A Strategy for Sustainable Living*, Gland, 1991.

World Resources Institute, *World Resources*, Oxford, New York, (published biennially).

SPECIAL REPORTS AND NEWSLETTERS

There is a large number of special reports, especially from governments, business, round tables, science and environment groups. They include updates on specific issues, such as the greenhouse effect, toxic chemicals, waste management, wildlife and sustainable development. The Centre for Our Common Future in Geneva regularly produces the Bulletin on what is happening on the sustainable development front around the world. Worldwatch Institute produces an annual State of the World report and periodic issues reports, while the World Resources Institute produces a biennial statistical report and analysis. The Warmer Bulletin in Britain focuses on waste issues.

PERIODICALS

These include, *ECODECISION, Worldwatch Magazine, New Scientist, Scientific American, Seasons, Nature Canada, Equinox and Harrowsmith*. There are often special sections on the environment by magazines such as *Maclean's, Time, Newsweek* and *National Geographic*.

INDEX

A

B

C

D

E

F

MESSAGE TO JOURNALISTS
ABOUT ENVIRONMENTAL EDUCATION

Covering the Environment was developed in conjunction with Environmental Issues for Journalists, a short course for working journalists held each year at the University of Western Ontario. This course, the first of its kind in Canada, is operated by the Centre for Mass Media Studies and Professional Development, Graduate School of Journalism. It is codirected by Michael Keating, an environment writer, and Professor Colin Baird of Western's Chemistry Department. Peter Desbarats, Dean of the Graduate School of Journalism, is overall supervisor.

The aim of the program is to give journalists accurate information on environment issues, and ideas on how to research and write environment stories that are both interesting and balanced. There are sessions on environmental issues, sustainable development and environmental journalism. Students spend a week in residence, and receive in depth lectures and background material from a wide range of experts. In addition to the co-directors, the lecturers have included the North American head of the United Nations Environment Programme, senior scientists, business leaders and heads of nongovernment organizations. The course is open to any full-time staff or freelance reporter or editor in newspapers, magazines, radio or television. The course is conducted in English, but there are no writing sessions, and the lectures are easily followed by francophones with a working knowledge of English. One of the co-directors is bilingual.

The program has support from a wide range of organizations, including business, government, nongovernment organizations and a foundation. It receives input from a Board of Advisors representing a wide spectrum of experience in environment and communications from across the country.

161

For more information about the Environmental Issues for Journalists program, please contact:

Office of the Dean
Graduate School of Journalism
Middlesex College
University of Western Ontario
London, Ontario N6A 5B7
Tel: (519) 661-3383   Fax: (519) 661-3848

or

Send the following page to
the Graduate School of Journalism at Western

ENVIRONMENTAL ISSUES FOR JOURNALISTS SHORT COURSE

For more information about the Environmental Issues for Journalists short course, please fill in this page and mail or fax it to the following address:

Office of the Dean
Graduate School of Journalism
Middlesex College
University of Western Ontario
London, Ontario N6A 5B7

Tel: (519) 661-3383   Fax: (519) 661-3848

**PLEASE SEND ME INFORMATION ABOUT
THE ENVIRONMENTAL ISSUES FOR JOURNALISTS COURSE.**

NAME _____

TITLE _____

EMPLOYER _____

ADDRESS _____

_____

_____

TEL _____   FAX _____

My experience with or interest in environment reporting:

_____

_____

_____

_____

PLEASE PHOTOCOPY THIS FORM

NRTEE MEMBERS